TABLE OF CONTENTS

ACKNOWLEDGEMENTS

I would like to thank Shabnam for always encouraging me and helping me to bring out the best in myself.

I would like to thank Chloe for working hand in hand with me on this book as she edited this book before it was anything official.

DEDICATION

This book is dedicated to all those who have suffered from mental illnesses from the past and present times. I hope you know that your suffering is not in vain. Through your suffering you have created hope and light for others.

The Grace of our Lord Jesus Christ be with you always.

1

REVELATION AND KNOWLEDGE

"But blessed are your eyes for they see, and your ears for they hear" - Matthew 13:16

I

Before every rainbow, there needs to be a terrible storm. Before every discovery there needs to be some sort of effort, some form of struggle, which reveals to us what path to take in life. Whether it be logical or a religious path, etc., we do not understand that which is presented before us, almost at first, but it is within our means to comprehend what we perceive, based on time and learning.

For ten years, I have struggled. For ten years, I have longed for answers. For ten years, I have been on the pursuit of happiness, fashioning my way through life. I managed to find some, although not all, but just enough, to enable me to grasp the concept of how we view things daily. It is by our mindset that we create our reality and therefore allow certain triggers to get underneath our skin and shape the way we feel.

Knowledge is greater than all. Knowledge is power.

II

I have experienced a great many things in life so far. Despite only being at the age of twenty-four, I feel as though life has fast-tracked me and matured me at a younger age, so that I can understand what I do now and in turn pass on knowledge which would grow me and in turn grow others. I feel that in some respects, I am ahead of my time in the way I understand and interpret the situations which are presented before me. This is my blessing and might also be my curse. I am yet to decide as I write.

Starting out with the diagnosis of depression at the age of fourteen, life had never been darker and I had never felt lonelier. How was it possible that a boy at such a young age would go through this? How did God allow this? Did I do something wrong for the notion of Karma to dish out to me what I deserved? Did I sin against my brother or neighbor in my past life? Or did I by some chance do all this to myself? Was I born cursed? Or did my parents not raise me correctly? All these thoughts, just to find out that a chemical imbalance in the brain was responsible for contemplating death.

I understand now that it was my brain which was responsible for me seeing dark clouds, despite being a sunny day. The dark clouds were in my head all along.

III

Yes, I suffered.

IV

Suffering does not always look like a physical ailment. It can just as well affect you by sneaking up into your head and rolling things around. It can just as much destroy your mind by perverting your perception on the things you sense. This is a mental affliction. Sometimes I wonder if physical or mental pain is worse than the other. I have not concluded that just yet.

I had a tiresome time managing high school and my social circle. Loneliness was my closest friend in my despair. It was closer than a physical human. I recall the anguish very much that afflicted me and even till this day, I get some taste of it. Only now of course, with years of battling, I understand how to deal with it.

Loneliness was made known to me and so was depression, anxiety, and all the negative feelings which I am now aware of had revealed itself to me. What I had not learnt yet, was how to overcome these things.

V

"For in much wisdom is much grief: and he that increaseth knowledge increaseth sorrow." - Ecclesiastes 1:18.

So, with the pain that I experienced, till now, I have learnt a multitude of lessons. The bible is right when it says that knowledge brings sorrow, but I have always wondered why that is the case. Isn't knowledge meant to result in power? Not in this case I suppose. However, it is a necessary tool to prepare a man to deal with the unexpected. Knowledge comes from many experiences and we know that life is the greatest teacher. We gain knowledge and revelation from daily life and its struggles. We also gain it through education and experiences on the field of life.

Back to my youth, I realized that I was feeling more and more alone. Where had this come from? All these feelings of negativity and destruction took me by surprise and not yet been given guidance on how to handle this situation. Despite this, I had to ride the wave. Not knowing whether it was going to get better, I still stuck to the path put in front of me and completed my secondary education.

My social circle was afflicted as these thoughts prevented me from forming and maintaining close relationships. My desires for wanting a girlfriend were destroyed by self- esteem issues. All I really wanted was to disappear somewhere else, even die. Everyone was better looking than me. I was not a handsome white guy with blue eyes, a nice body and wavy surfer hair. I was brown, ethnic and looked like I was fresh of the boat. Nobody wants to date that.

Now I understand how social circles work, what people desire, how to be desirable and most of all, what people expect from others. This caused my perception of others to become more negative as I realised that I felt more of an outcast simply due to the assumptions that no girl wanted me. Hell, I didn't even want me! How did I expect a girl to want me when I didn't even want myself? I didn't want to be an Indian bloke from SINGAPORE, I wanted to be whatever handsome was, so long as I had blue eyes and girls liked me.

It can be quite exhausting really, having to feel left out in a society of good-looking people, but I managed to ride the wave and gain more and more understanding of the way the teenage world worked. And with more knowledge, further sorrows pierced my soul.

VI

Every night I prayed 'Jesus, make me look good'. I accepted Christ and converted into Christianity a year after I started learning how bad things could get, simply because I wanted things to get better and I had no one else to turn to. "Come to church and receive Jesus, He will make things better", a friend had invited me.

"Well, why not? If it helps, then sure", the same answer I gave when the idea of anti-depressants was placed on the table before me. I went to church, learnt again, received Christ, learnt more. Nothing happened.... on the spot. Back to riding the wave I go.

Things got worse, and I prayed. Did you know that you can pray for wisdom and knowledge and that the Bible encouraged us to do so? I PRAYED! And prayed and prayed. "God, make things to get better! Give me a reason to live!" I cried.

Still riding the wave here.

I pressed on as the days seemed endless and gloomier. I relied heavily upon Christianity to teach me that everything was going to be alright and I was under mentorship (even till this day) from an advanced Christian. I looked out for the knowledge that would help me to live life to the best of my ability and to remain in good spirits. Based on Christian values, one had to draw close to God and remain faithful to the church, yet, it seemed that I was not acquiring a satisfactory spiritual return. I did not feel the peace that I had expected.

But I learnt more and more I learnt.

VII

I began to commit myself to psychology sessions. Their purpose was to assist me in delving into the root cause of my mental conflict and uprooting whatever mess was brewing inside. As I saw them frequently, I began to start questioning myself. For the first time in my life, I experience self-doubt and I awakened the explorer within myself. I started to ask God why I was going through such a perilous journey at a young age. I was so overwhelmed with suicide that I resorted to self-harm in order to find release. Let me tell you that it does not work. I saw in the mirror a shattered individual in his youth who had already lost hope in life, and it had not even started. Life was not even official for a young student for myself and I wanted it all to end.

The concept of trial and error is a marvellous thing which encourages indefinite learning and further wisdom. The psychological term of trial and error according to Oxford Languages is "the process of experimenting with various methods of doing something until one finds the most successful." Sounds a bit like the definition of insanity does it not? It is a fundamental method of problem solving and the key is to find the most appropriate solution. People may think that you waste time and miss out when you do not achieve the desired outcome, but I think that you learn something regardless from each proposed outcome. You build a greater understanding of what you set out to achieve and begin to realise why you aspire to succeed in what you want to achieve. These thoughts start to captivate your mind and you begin to constantly apply these ideas to your basic life and dream about how deep you may aspire with the possibility of success.

Psychologically, another way of learning is through the observations of others. We observe the behaviours and reactions of others, and subconsciously tend to mimic their way of doing things. We start to realise the potential rewards from learned behaviours and we find comfort in that. We adopt various opinions towards the norms of society. We strive to be like others. Conformity is something that we partake in when we realise how left out we are, or think we are. This constitutes further mimicry and we tend to lose our original views on the way of life before our minds conformed.

I had decided that if I wanted to be cool, I needed to fit in with the crowd. High school was a breeding ground for conformists and observational learning. After all you didn't know any better than what your peers thought should be good for you.

I learnt that to be a part of something bigger, one had to conform to the ideas of the majority. Sleeping with more girls made you a bigger man. It was something to bring to the table and show off whilst every teenager around you went "wooahhh". Or getting drunk and doing backflips into the pool made you an idol amongst the maturing teenagers. If you weren't part of the cool kids, you're a loser and you had to feel ashamed of yourself. God knows I did. Being a 'cool kid' or a 'loser' were the only options there were – we believed.

VIII

Alas, having a different perspective was the only way to save my emotions. What the general population thought was cool, I had to label as "sin". What they were getting up to, to me, they were going to screw up their lives, they were going to hell. I had to understand that for me to thrive and move on, and to not succumb to the social norms, I had to take the mature approach and see that even I was doing important things, which they may potentially not matter in years down the track.

Yes, I adopted this the hard way, through much grief and isolation, knowing that I mattered little and thinking that every step in the right direction may result in little to no change in my future. Knowing that I was a sad wreck of a loser, who would amount to nothing in early life, just because I hadn't slept with someone yet.

Boy oh boy, poor me. What a shame that I had to bear. The overwhelming burden of not having enough popularity, nor possessing the power to seduce ladies with my words and looks. All of this, did not matter. I realised years later, had I understood what it all counted for in the end, I would not have troubled myself with these woes for I know now I was made for something better. The perspective of the rapidly developing brain of an average teenage boy will sooner or later understand what is important and what is not. I began to realise, but only through pain and disappointment.

Although the law establishes that you reach a mature age of eighteen in most countries, or even twenty-one in others, scientists have established that the rational part of a teen's brain isn't fully developed and won't be until age twenty-five or so.

This impacts the thinking and rational perception of the person. Individuals trust in activities which exercise their brains and thinking capacity, for there are a lot of methods which contribute to the growth of the brain.

Scientists established that adult and teenagers' brains work differently. Adults think with the prefrontal cortex, the brain's rational part. This is the part of the brain that responds to situations with good judgment and an awareness of long-term consequences. Teens process information with the amygdala which is the emotional part.

In teens' brains, the connections between the emotional part of the brain and the decision-making centre are still developing—and not always at the same rate. That's why when teens have overwhelming emotional input, they can't explain later what they were thinking. They weren't thinking as much as they were feeling.

Events such as childhood trauma can drastically alter the behaviour and development of teens. Childhood trauma causes unwanted reaction to minor triggers. People tend to be sensitive to small situations. This is because the trauma experienced by people causes the amygdala to be oversensitive to any perception of threats encountered. The responses which incite fear in people are triggered easily as time passes.

People make their decisions based on the emotions created from the situations they encounter. For example, attempting suicide because I don't have enough friends or wanting to slit my wrists because someone doesn't value me enough. All for the sake of wanting to follow my heart, when my brain can't even keep up. They say to follow your heart but I say to be rational. Think before you do and take all the time with thinking. Better to be safe than sorry.

You never know what you can do to yourself or others when your feelings get in the way. You might cause unnecessary conflicts or issues for yourself. You might confuse yourself and ultimately make the wrong decision for yourself. Ask yourself whether it is worth it or not. Understand the biological side of things, but also ensure that the logical side of things is in play. YOU, in your essence and being, are in charge after all.

IX

When I speak of the word "revelation", I think of the final book in the New Testament in the Bible. When I make mere mention of this word, people around me relate it to a religious context. When I learn about something new, does it mean that it is divine? I agree most certainly, coming from a faith-filled background, but there also is the concept of self-discovery and revelation in daily lives. Revelation, according to religion, is caused by the disclosure of divine or sacred reality or purpose to humanity. Through faith and religious concepts, such disclosure may come through mystical insights, historical events, or spiritual experiences that transform the lives of individuals and groups. When the disciples saw Jesus Christ transfigured into God's glory on the Mount; or when Buddha attained enlightenment under the Bodhi tree, or when the Prophet Mohammed received the Qur'an from Allah, through the angel Jibril on the Night of Power, or even when Hindus received their religion through the Vedas which are direct intuitional revelations and are held to be Apaurusheya or entirely superhuman, without any author in particular; it has been appropriated that these are various examples of revelation in action. Revelations are highly regarded and revered as they are seen to be the keys of solving all the problems or answering all the questions in life. The answers which solve all the world's problems and answer all the world's questions.

I did not realize that I would have to work out my own path and some answers were meant to be revealed later in life. I was naïve and I thought that my problems could be fixed in an instant. Till this day, I sometimes slide into the mindset of wanting to have everything fixed instantly and I forget that patience is a virtue.

Without the religious viewpoint, if I were to discover how to solve a problem in my life without divine intervention, it would still be considered a revelation, because it is an act of realization, in my mind and my being, that there is some way to achieve and overcome the obstacles presented before me.

I still have to look for answers till this day but I know that it is about the journey of self- discovery which in turn leads to self-growth. Each circumstance or each obstacle has a specific solution to it that is not exactly the same as other obstacles. I learnt that the hard way. We have to always be ready to apply a new method of problem solving, whether it be in your head or in a physical manifestation throughout life. Every problem has their length in time but it is up to you how long it remains in your life.

I have realized, that despite the lack of training in certain fields, one can still understand and partake in any knowledge if one is affronted with the situations that create revelation, such as adversity. Adversity can be a friend when one approaches challenges with delight and the eagerness to learn. I understand that for one to grow, their being must be stretched and moulded, broken and reshaped, destroyed for something stronger and newer to take its place. Based on the perspective of the wise man, he embraces a challenge so that his mind can be widened to the knowledge and understanding of the way life works. Plain and simple.

X

Earlier on I mentioned that knowledge is power. Is knowledge worth more than money? How does it make one more powerful? Is it the key to living a successful and healthy life? Do you save yourself a lot of heartache? The answer is yes. At this point in time, as I write to you, dear reader, yes. Yes. Knowing a lot, knowing what can happen, reading the situation ahead, can save you so much of pain and dread and heartache. I wish that I knew all the things that I know now before I had jumped into the deep end. To avoid the things that were lurking beneath the deep dark waters to snatch away my identity and my persona. To give myself opportunities to avoid a lifetime of regret, even though I am only twenty-four. I wish I had done more with certain people. I wish I had not lost myself in certain occasions. I wish I made the right choices financially so that I would have so much money saved up by now. I wish that I had valued and fought for certain friendships. All of this I would have done, if I had the better knowledge to guide me.

I now strive to prepare myself and to base my learnings from the experiences that other people have had and gone through. Especially when they confide in and share with me, I have determined that I am to accept full counsel and advice from my peers and value the advice that people give me. I wish I had listened to my parents more. They are further experienced than I am and have lived through greater experiences. They were able to read certain situations I was caught up in and warned me of the dangers if I continued in them, as though they were prophets, but really, they had been through something similar before and understood the consequences. They were trying to save me a world of trouble, if only I listened. Although I learned a lot the hard way, I am looking for myself daily and learning the way of the ever-evolving world. This in turn builds perspective and contributes to the state of mind that people choose to have. For better or worse: I have chosen for better.

I write to you earnestly to divulge the information that I have learnt in order that you would know that there is more to life than knowing what you know. That by gaining knowledge and revelation, you would learn to live your best life. Do what makes you happy and promotes your peace of mind, if you are doing things the right way. Keep others before you and ask them about their lives. Spread good will and cheer. Be there for others. Share your experiences and give advice freely. Through the simple acts of kindness, you will learn what engages people and what turns people away. By becoming more aware of this, you also learn how to engage with people. Your social skills are developed and you have no reason to have social anxieties nor worries that might otherwise grip and hold you down. It is good to be the life of the crowd and someone for people to turn to. People like that are invaluable.

Recognise that you can learn, through documentaries, through travel (I learnt a lot in my time in India), through faith, through grandparents, through heartache and pain, through work and education. In whatever way you can, absorb the energies of your surroundings, wherever you place your feet. There will always be a point of despair but I showed myself that if you can turn around bad for good, then you can survive anything. I question myself daily to search for the meaning of life. I continuously search for the importance in myself and in my journey. I do not always find the answers but I must continue to push on to a new level of self-discovery.

> *"They will be like a tree planted by the **water** that sends out its roots by the stream. It does not fear when heat comes; its leaves are always green. It has no worries in a year of drought and never fails to bear fruit»- Jeremiah 17:7-8.*

2

THE JOURNEY THAT MADE ME

"The Lord will keep you from all harm- he will watch over your life; the Lord will watch over your coming and going, both now and forevermore"- Psalm 121:7-8

I

Like a hollowed-out silhouette; I walk the face of this planet pondering on what physical or spiritual elements that I can fill my soul with. I strive in the pursuit of knowledge, education and career elements that can help me to feel full in my heart and gratify the innards of my being. However, I still walk with the sense of a dark void within me, hungering to devour nourishing elements that my surroundings can offer me. To satisfy the soul is a much more difficult task than I could have possibly imagined. The longing to be enveloped in love and fulfillment is such a hungering that takes over my priorities and causes my mind to focus on what I do not have, rather than what I have attained.

It is almost as though a curse of hunger has enveloped my being and I feel lost almost daily, wondering and hoping about what I can use to fill myself. To fill my needs, I look for meaningful relationships and love. I seek the joys of living simply. I strive to make a difference in the lives of others if it means that my life becomes meaningful and that I feel fulfilled. Although I may make a difference to something in one day, the next day the hunger returns. It is a curse that I am never fully nourished nor filled with what I need.

My mind revolves daily on ways that I can allow what fills me to last longer, so that my satisfaction can endure over a long period of time; until I find something else to fill me. Nothing lasts forever so I find myself in an everlasting search for meaning and soulful nourishment. It is a strenuous task that I have to see myself through on an almost daily basis. What has my life come to?

Earlier I talked about the time of my early youth; revolving my high school life. In the year 2015, I, at the age of eighteen, had graduated from high school with flying colours. I had doubts about making it this far as I feared my emotions would get the better of me and cause me to fail. The preparation from school life to "real" life was astounding. I contemplated fiercely on achieving my dreams and I had inscribed in my heart, the path that I was going to take. That was the path I was going to dedicate myself to, no matter what the cost. It was a blissful experience.

All of us were ready to get out of our shells and take on what life had to offer us. Preparing ourselves for the real world ahead. The only problem was, like most kids, I was naïve about what I had to do. I defied the reality of life and pursued after my goals in a dream like vision. A lot of us don't really get out of that state until we encounter something that tears us apart from within, and only then we realise the genuine reality of life.

The grass isn't always greener on the other side. We attempt to defy the laws of life by having dreamy goals and vision, but what we do not consider, is that, while we reside on this planet, we are subject to the reality of things and we must adhere to realistic steps in order to become something.

By remaining in a dreamy state, we close ourselves to all acquirable knowledge because we think we know everything. That is truly where the danger lies.

I felt like I could achieve more as I approached the final years of my high school life. I determined to acquire the respect of my teachers by being a model student in the school council and showed kindness and offered to be a friend to friends who needed someone. I discovered some form of satisfaction when I realized I could be there to help people as we all were a developing bunch of teens with raging emotions. I targeted those who were involved in high school issues and offered myself before them. The more I reached out to, the more I felt that I was important. The more I helped others, the more I believed that I would be satisfied within myself. Still, the void lingered and continued to haunt me.

As I reached out to people, I decided to expand my circle of friends. I wanted to be more included in peoples' lives so that I could subconsciously remind them that I existed. I only wanted things to feel better for myself. I shared my own issues with other people as well and found only a few that I could relate to. The hunger for importance continued as I shared more of myself around. I carried on until I realized that I was not taking care of myself and all of a sudden, it all came crashing down. The void in my soul tapped me on the shoulder and reminded me that it was still lingering in me. Like a vampire drawn to blood, I sought to fill the cravings of feeling important but I could not always get it immediately. There was only so much I could do and I only could do my best with what I had.

High school was a time where I was developing myself and learning more about myself. As the void in me grew, my insecurities grew and I felt that I could not always reach out to be there for others. I was ignoring myself and I did not know how to look after myself. It was tiring to always look out for others and I felt it would be a strong relief to relax myself in the considerations and concern of others and I desired once again that I required love. I reminded myself that I wanted to be important and I started again in desiring the feeling of acceptance from others.

I graduated high school but it did not satisfy me. Now I was plunged into the open world and I felt I was lacking a whole lot more. I had more reasons to be scared and nervous as I was now in the real world where people did not care. The friends I relied on to feel important had went on their own paths, naturally, after graduation. I understood that everyone else wanted to make their own life and I wanted the same for myself. However, I felt a weight on me to progress and create something new. That weight was the same emptiness I discovered when I was fourteen. Now I was alone in the real world and I had to focus on looking after myself more than ever.

II

I received the news, straight after high school, by the laws of my birthplace: Singapore; that I was required to enlist in two years of mandatory service of national defence of the country. National Service is what it is called and still occurs till this day. Boys who become men. At the age of eighteen, all male born citizens of Singapore are required to answer this call of duty and the service term ranges from twenty-two to twenty-four months. The vocations are: army, navy, air force, police or fire fighters.

I prepared myself mentally for the road ahead, unknowing of what was to come and how things were going to be. Where was I going to end up? What was I going to do in a home that seemed so foreign to myself? Having been away since 2008, at the age of eleven when my parents moved to Australia. Unsure of whether I was going to adjust well, I still challenged myself to answer the call and went ahead with it.

I left Melbourne in January 2016 and embarked on a journey of a lifetime, which till this day, I hate and appreciate at the same time. I gathered my wits and landed in Singapore; excited as ever and ready to take on what was going to come my way. Not realising the reality of what was to come, I was ready to take any situation head on.

III

"Blessed be the LORD my Rock, Who traineth my hands for war, And my fingers for battle..." -Psalm 144:1

There I was, a stranger in what was my place of birth. I was getting accustomed to my immediate surrounds but I seemed to navigate myself around the island/state very well. Most of what I perceived, I managed to recall from my childhood so I was hardly lost. I drew the short straw and enlisted in the army in August 2016. Prior to that, I had contacted friends and family back home to inform them of my placement and they were excited for me. I was excited for myself. I knew that being in the army would look good on my resume for when I got back home and pursued my career choices. I considered all the benefits of being in the army that would assist me in progressing my life.

Somehow, despite the distractions of what was to come, the darkness had followed me to this new land, where I did not gain any peaceful sojourn. The feelings of loneliness and emptiness, up until my enlistment, were frequent, but now it was more difficult as everyone I knew was back home and only some family members were around. The thoughts of death that ravaged my mind, forcing my hand to attempt the unspeakable, was frequent but I had managed to fight them by attempting to make new friends and keeping in touch with some family. However, it was not enough. I'm not sure how but I managed to persevere and made it to enlistment day, where I felt that I finally had reached my purpose and that I would be doing something fruitful for the nation and for myself.

Upon enlistment, I prepared everything that was required of me. The Ministry of Defence had ensured that I received the location to attend with the correct itinerary and inventory. My father had flown down to send me off and watch me as I marched off with the new recruits into the training grounds. I recall the smouldering heat of that day as we had waved goodbye to our loved ones and marched off in formation to the trucks that would lead us to our camps.

This was a taste of the upcoming responsibility and adult life that I was to take part in. My mind had not prepared for being broken down and remoulded into the mindset of a soldier. At first, I was lost but then things began to crumble down in my being. I was not just being prepared to defend the country, but I learnt quickly that I had to learn to defend my mind from the darkness that could potentially destroy me.

It was time to prove myself as a man to society and to those who expected this of me. The commanders saw to that swiftly, upon entering the camp, that we who knew not what we were expected to carry out, were instructed in the ways of responsible and militarized men. The spirit of a soldier was carved into my spirit and with the training at hand, we were ready to take on anything and anyone that dared enter conflict with our proud nation.

IV

The downfall came out of nowhere and it drastically changed how I began to perceive the world. It had begun in the early weeks of the army training. I can scarcely recall the exact moment in which I was triggered but I do recall it was by roughly the fourth day of my army enlistment. As recruits, we were getting settled and still being oriented about life in the camp. The requirements of us were instilled without fail by our commanders.

I was not nervous but going with the flow of the days as they went by but there was an inner urge to fight against being detained. There was a side of me that disagreed strongly with the idea of being here against my free will. I felt estranged in the desolate camp, in the likes of a prisoner. I had begun to feel certain thoughts of loneliness and isolation creep in my mind.

As much as I tried to dispel them by focusing on the goals at hand, they seemed to overpower my thoughts and my emotions began to erupt within me. I felt as though I was driven by emotions rather than logic as I felt certainly out of place. It was the immediate realization that I was not supposed to be here, amongst the other trainees, which threw me off and desperately wanted to escape the reality of the remaining two years.

I felt as though a stranger despite my army mates. No amount of "gung-ho" army values could distract me as I needed to be back home in Australia. It was then I realized the value of family and friends back home in Australia. The training continued nonetheless and so did the dark thoughts. Now I started to feel as a zombie, despite carrying out the routines of the daily training. We began at five in the morning and ended at roughly ten in the evening.

All throughout, the only thing I could focus on were the thoughts on escaping and not wanting to be here. The loneliness and isolation pressed down on my shoulders and eventually my spirit broke. I hoped that my life would account for more and that my desire for importance would be met through the service of my home country. I felt the exact opposite as I was just a number and felt like another body to throw in the defence of a nation.

Where was the sense of importance when I was supposed to be at the pivotal point of a nation's defence? I felt like a regular grunt as I marched and participated in the drills prepared in our training. I tried to envision myself being some sort of important figure in the army. It didn't happen.

The void continued to grow as I sat on the parade square polishing my rifle. With a weapon in my hand, it would have been nice to put a bullet through my eyes. That way, at least I would never have to feel the sorrow of emptiness ever again.

V

'I needed help! And I needed it now'. In the army culture, having these thoughts and emotions was a sign of weakness. I had succumbed to the thoughts of suicide whilst in camp and I had never felt so broken. I was an empty machine, carrying out the training throughout the day but every second I thought of death and despair. Eventually, it was found out amongst my commanders that I was not coping and was referred to an army counsellor. I later discovered that I had "adjustment issues". The name holds the obvious meaning.

The downward spiral which caught me off guard now had a name and it haunted me daily and nightly. I was then excused from the basic training, diagnosed with this "weakness" and excused from the training. I was redeployed into another camp and that was the last I saw my initial army mates. How much of a disappointment I must have been?

VI

Months pressed on and settling into my new vocation in the army intelligence logistics department proved to be a smoother adjustment. Aside from the army I was given leave every day at five in the evening to go home and was required to report back the next morning at eight. My vocation was operated during weekdays and I had the weekend off as well.

Aside from the army I took this opportunity to refresh myself and explore Singapore. I set out time to visit some family members and caught up with some of my newfound friends. Despite this I still felt lonely, not as much as before, but it was still there. There were those dark days, however they were not as frequent. I took every chance to keep myself busy, lest my mind should become idle. That was the first time I learnt that being idle and bored could be a doorway for a lot of negative mental thoughts and issues.

My brain is always flickering with thoughts and this has its positives and negatives. I long for opportunities to keep myself busy and found it difficult to succumb into rest and free times.

To combat this, I had to adjust my perception of the world. I still struggle with this till today but I have learnt that keeping busy can be an ultimate path to bask in fulfillment and joy.

Being idle provokes the mind into diving into foolish thoughts. I learnt that I could have avoided a lot of thoughts had I kept myself busy. Had I kept myself focused on something; I would have saved myself a lot of pain. However, this is not always the case because sometimes, the circumstances are not in favour of your joy and there is essentially nothing at all to do. Even with these cards I was dealt, I had to formulate a way to play them in my favour.

Boredom is one of my greatest enemies and I realised that I had to mould my mind to combat these thoughts with uttering out loud what my focus was. Sometimes I had to utter my focuses multiple times for my mind to reset on the goals at hand.

The misconception of the world around us can also be changed by uttering your goals, therefore changing your perspective on how you want things to be, rather than allowing circumstance to win over you. The world is cruel and you need to be able to fight it. It is not an easy task, but nothing is ever easy if you are pressing in the right direction. Sometimes you must fight for your own sanity by reinforcing yourself with positive nourishment.

We pick up the energy around us, and if things seem negative or boring, we must physically relocate ourselves to another location where there are positive vibes. Then, we ought to reconfigure our minds on what we desire to see in ourselves and then utter these goals or changes and press on.

Believe me, it is easier said than done. But I had a lot of time to practise.

VII

"And let us run with perseverance the race marked out for us...."- Hebrews 12:1

As I approached the one-year mark of my service term, I decided to congratulate myself on making it this far. I longed for my service to be accomplished and I set my mind to completing the final year and longed for to embark on the journey home. I attained two promotions which kept me fuelled in my journey and I used these events as positive reminders.

When you establish positive reminders, people may celebrate them with you but there is a special power in it when you celebrate it most. You understand the depth of your achievements and this gives you the mental strength to push forward unto completion.

Despite the time I had served and the achievements which I celebrated, I still felt isolated and left out in this foreign world. I watched inquisitively as the people of this land go by about their day, mingling with friends and loved ones and I longed for that feeling of belonging. Although I had friends, I still felt trapped within my inner bubble of loneliness and I needed to break out to join the crowd.

Feeling isolated is a deadly thorn in your side. It can grip you immensely and contribute to the negative thoughts of dying. A common factor of suicide is due to isolation. We as humans, long for the company of others as an innate necessity and we thrive off the energy off others to keep us functioning. I seemed to be at a lack of this and this threw me off immensely.

I began to doubt myself and question my life. How much longer was I required to endure this; I did not know for certain. Despite being aware of the time I had till I left and went home, it felt as though I was trapped here forever. In all honesty, the only way of dealing with this was constant communication. It could not be provided all the time as others had to go on with their lives. However, where the opportunity presented itself, I took it. In the times of my lonesome, I had to constantly reassure myself that I was going to be alright. This was where I began to develop anxiety. I was constantly worried about being alone but the best way to conquer your fears is to face them.

I decided that I had to deal with being alone, and I had learnt from certain people that being alone with yourself was not necessarily a bad thing but it was a time to reflect and to rediscover yourself. I practised this and it allowed me the opportunity to identify my strengths and weakness. In the areas I lacked, I had the chance to provide for myself and build upon the things that held me back, mentally.

Practising self-reflection is time consuming in a good way and can be a vital tool in progressing yourself in life. However, too much time alone can be damaging. I learnt to spend time with myself and take myself out to discover new things in my surroundings. Whilst doing so, I had to mentally reassure myself that it was alright to be alone. In this sense, I managed my anxiety and sub consciously, you will not be aware of how much stronger you get as a person and this is a sort of independence that you achieve.

VIII

I completed my army service in August 2018 and I could not have been more proud of myself. It was time to go back to Australia and begin my life as an adult. As I mentioned about self-reflection earlier, I utilise this till this day and there are always times that I think I could have done things differently. I am still learning and refuse to stop learning.

We as humans tend to fall into the bitter pit of regret occasionally. I had to master my mind in this field as well by accepting and making peace with the past and by letting go. It can take time as there are some things which I am learning to let go of till this day. I determined that the journey and it turned out that the troubles I experienced with my surroundings had shaped me into the person I am today and I was able to walk away from it with lessons and with the knowledge ready to change my perception of the world.

I had altered my state of mind through knowledge and what better way to learn than by being thrown into the deep end. What seemed as a curse at that time revealed itself to be a blessing in disguise. The mental wars that were forged almost daily in my mind could not compare to the victory I had felt when I completed what I thought impossible at the time.

I doubted myself multiple times by saying that I was never going to finish my term: I was either going to drop out dishonourably or end up taking my own life.

Commitment is a strong force when manipulated by the strong mind. It is with great urge that I encourage those who commit to things to see it through to the day of completion. One must train and discipline their mind to set their eyes on the rewards, despite the obstacles at hand. Motivation is a unique driving force which must also be discovered for one to persevere.

All of us require a reason to fulfil certain things but the reason is not always given at the start. It is through these toils, sometimes, in which we discover these reasons and then should make the necessary choices.

I urge you to be disciplined and convicted in setting out to do the things you do. I battled suicidal thoughts, loneliness, isolation and anxiety in a foreign land and I managed to do something that I never thought I could do.

The human mind can be changed to adapt to different situations, like a sponge that is able to be scrunched up, stretched and bent; yet still retain its original shape. It needs to be fed with positive experiences and negatives views can be corrected within the challenges it faces.

You are just as strong and can do all that you aspire to do. If you do not have a reason, look in the mirror, YOU are the reason.

3

THE DARKNESS

"Even the darkness is not dark to You, And the night is as bright as the day. Darkness and light are alike to You" – Psalm 139:12

I

The darkness that I speak about is not physical but mental. Falling into the darkness is a state of mind. It is an infinitely deep abyss filled with all that the human mind refuses to acknowledge as real and attempts to flee from. The darkness is overwhelming and can chew you up without hesitation. The darkness doesn't discriminate. It comes after whoever that is weak enough to welcome it. It hides itself as a wolf amongst the sheep and pounces on its unwary target, leaving behind a trail of pain and destruction. It is like an infection, to which there is no cure. It is like bad fruit, that rots and rots till it is discarded. The darkness lingers in the darker parts of the human mind and the soul. It is something that conjures up out of its own will and requires immense will to pacify.

The darkness has no mercy nor does it have remorse. Its intent is to destroy that which it seeks out to devour and to manipulate people into weakness. It is an affliction unlike any other and must not be underestimated. We must understand that this is a force which must not be taken lightly. It is to be taken seriously as a physical ailment for this is one which afflicts the mind and spirit. It weakens the will of the victim and isolates their mind from all that is bright and positive.

We are in a fragile world with much to despair. The darkness roams freely and wherever it goes, it annihilates any pure and perfect environment. We are susceptible to its touch and must take heed of every sign it displays for us not to be provoked by it. It is a challenge that we must each face as it comes for us at different times of our lives. When confronted, we must approach it with steadfastness and resilience, lest it overtakes our soul.

II

As human beings, we are put through a range of emotions and thoughts daily. We partake in the things which give us joy and on that which causes grief. Each day, we are put through these things and we learn to adapt to the patterns of our emotional triggers. We discover what is necessary for us and what we must avoid. We attempt with different tactics, to overcome the darker aspects of life to better ourselves. We are not always prepared and complacency comes without cause. In this sense, the darkness tends to have a certain hold over us, in which it always resides in us, and when provoked, we experience the downward spiral in which it so cruelly puts us through.

What was originally known as Melancholia: Depression is an oppressive mental health illness which is often known to be caused by chemical imbalances in the brain and causes the symptoms of low moods, not being motivated, loss of interest and various other impairments in an individual's daily life. The thoughts of suicidal ideation are frequent and the path towards escape grows narrower. The light seems to grow dimmer and the hope of escape is all but lost. It is an affliction unlike any other and the results of it are horrific. You'd end up losing relationships and destroying opportunities in life. You'd end up turning to narcotics as a means of escape. There are numerous physical causes for depression. Ranging from: marriage breakdowns to loneliness and isolation in society, to mental aspects such as a simple chemical imbalance in your brain which can fluctuate your moods without your control. Otherwise known as "mood swings" or "bipolar". As you lay in bed wide awake, there is a weight that presses your chest down and you find it difficult to kick start the day and conduct your day-to-day activities. There is no motivation to do anything anymore! Worst of all, all you desire is death. The destruction of your own being is brought on by depression, which can cause suicidal behaviour and ideation.

Your spiritual eyes are covered by an invisible scale. You can't see anything anymore. You are blinded by the very things that seek to destroy your soul. You are plunged into a pit of darkness where there is bitter agony. Abandon all hope. It feels like hell. It has felt like hell to me ever since. You are blinded from seeing the love that family and friends have for you. You are locked away in a shell which is internalized. That shell is created by you subconsciously as a way to cope but you will realize sooner or later that it does more damage to your mind than good.

Sitting in the dark eventually forces you to search for the light. I was forced to crawl my way out of that horrendous shell which I sought to live in. I knew that eventually I had to do something about the negativity I was forced to live with. I had to rise above my brooding to be someone who had the guts to accept what I was going through and find ways in which I could cope healthily. I had to make use of the faith stirring up in me to seek the light. If I could not, I had to at least create the light. I had to create some hope for myself that one day I would achieve a positive state of mind and meet my desire for happiness and serenity.

To some avail, there are behavioural therapies and various treatments including medication to assist in dealing with these moods. It is a challenge that people face at some part in their life. I have explored and researched further into this and I have discussed with people who are oppressed by this. There are many who have confided and confessed that they have gone through this and that they feel rather sad instead of joy. Their reasons are usually similar and I suspect that it is due to the location and its environment which is one main cause. The weather also affects the moods but usually it is the environment in which they reside in.

People are conflicting with this almost daily, utilising tools such as psychological and medical assistance to assist them. Some of these battles stretch out for years. There is a danger in not being up front with these emotions and one must be transparent with their own self. Confronting them is the first step in overcoming them. Accept that you have these ailments and make peace with your circumstances. You need to explore methods of overcoming this persecution; either professionally or through your own means. The most important thing is that you believe in yourself to overcome.

III

Anxiety is a common phenomenon experienced by most people which causes excessive worrying and panic. The body responds with physical symptoms to what the mind perceives as a threat. In this case, anxiety is caused from the heightened amount of thoughts which is caused by one's tendency to overthink. It is a dangerous sensation that causes an unsolicited amount of panic and fear which can drive people to cower for no reason. It is as though the darkness has a hold over the person who fears most.

The thing that drives anxiety is a lack of control of the mind and the emotions. It is also a disorder which involves the mental aspect of people. Certain personality types are more prone to this disorder as compared to others. Other times it can be a hormonal issue or simply due to the chemistry of the brain. Whatever the cause, anxiety is a gripping disorder which does not let go so easily.

The epitome of anxiety can come from trauma as many people have faced this in some way or another. Those who have been confronted with different types of abuse begin to develop trauma and in turn; this disorder, especially younger people.

For those who are traumatised, professional medical assistance is needed which enables one to receive coping strategies to manage their anxieties and symptoms.

IV

Isolation is a devastating circumstance whereby someone is excluded away from others to reside by themselves with their own thoughts. It brings forth the feelings of loneliness, contributes to anxieties and in the long run can phase out into depression. You do not need to be far from home to experience this. Sometimes, you can even experience this whilst you are in the company of others. You may start to feel alone whilst being in your community. The notion of isolation produces an invisible barrier around you, cutting you off from those around you. When you are not physically alone, you might feel it coming on from the mental state of your mind.

There are various factors to isolation. Being an outcast is a common feeling and it has caught me off guard. Although you may relate to people easily and be a very social person, you can still succumb to the feelings of loneliness. Every human being desires for the need of being included in some community or cultural group. Being alone for long periods of time can contribute to various stressors and mental spirals.

I have witnessed the long-term effects of loneliness and it can cause the victim to deteriorate mentally. For those who are afflicted with old age or disability, they are frequently affected with loneliness as they are viewed as people who cannot contribute to society, nor can they commit themselves to any career. These are the social outcasts which struggle in society and are prone to premature death.

I felt a sense of isolation when I was away in the army. It was a feeling of immense loneliness that came upon me and I started to think as though I was all alone in the world. The feeling of it is overwhelming and can be difficult to bear and the only way out of it is through communication with others. For those who have gone through it, it is vital to ensure that others do not go through it as well. It is so crippling that it removes the hope and joy out of someone rapidly, leaving the person feeling unwanted, discarded and empty.

<h2 style="text-align:center">V</h2>

"And let us not grow weary of doing good, for in due season we will reap, if we do not give up." – Galatians 6:9

If such examples of darkness run amuck, then there must be the light to combat it. It does not justify the fact that people can be easily affected without help being available. There are ways out for people and it can be reached, but these methods for help must be taught and must be readily available.

I feel that there is not enough help in this world, due to the selfishness of human nature. It feels as though it is every person for themselves and the world gives off the impression that if you are rich and famous, only then do people care about you. Only then are you valued and your name is remembered. For those who have opportunity to do good, they must readily provide that assistance to those who need it. Not everyone can make a name for themselves or allow themselves to be in the spotlight of the world. It is simply not practical. People long to feel special and we are here as humans to touch lives and make a difference to one another through inspiring change and good values.

It is human nature to rely on others when in times of trouble and such needs should be met. If they are not always met, there must be an effort of outreach from the community or from allocated groups. I do not see why people must struggle alone. Yes, it is a cruel world, but it does not have to remain as such. People wish to stand out from others and one way to do so is by spreading good and carrying out actions in love.

I am aware that we cannot control the actions of other people, nor can we force upon someone the values and necessity of being kind. We can only inspire and teach, with hopes that those who are determined to do the right thing, will grasp the value of doing good and persevere in kindness towards others.

For those who have not been appreciated, the views of others do not determine your worth for there are numerous ways in which you can make yourself aware of how special and unique you are. You are as important as you allow yourself to be. It would be most beneficial for one to recognise their gifts within themselves and use them to find themselves and their place in this world.

Do you realize who you are? Have you been made aware of what feats you are capable of? We are capable of more than we can imagine. Our trials and tribulations cause us to rise up stronger and emerge with indefinite wisdom. Depression does not, and will not define you, if you do not let it. I did not realize that I could make that stand. I had no idea that I could reject the image that depression portrayed over me.

We as humans serve a purpose and we must understand that, despite there being a higher power, we also have the power in our hands to create a ripple in the ways of the world. Each person is powerful enough, when in the right space to make a difference for good. It only takes motivation and being determined enough to provide that goodness.

When you have the right intentions at heart, with the right attitude, values and qualifications, you notice a change in your perspective towards the world. You start wanting more from the world. You start expecting there to be changes. Not everything will be smooth sailing in this world where there are constant rocky tides. My advice to you is to be the change. It is a common and well-known phrase; which all who desire to change the world should have it written in their hearts. Endeavour to be inspiring and make room for there to be goodness and love. That is how you envision change.

I have come to the enlightenment that it is up to ourselves to give ourselves the importance that we so deserve. We do not have to always feel so empty and without meaning if we put ourselves in the service of others in our work life or family life. We receive the appreciation through others because we allow our light to shine.

Your state of mind will be accustomed to the light as you will bear witness to the successes of being helpful. These successes will act as testimonies and will encourage others to partake during change.

I learnt that happiness is a choice so now I had to look for the strength to make the choice daily and find things to be happy about. It was recommended to me by various people in life to create a list of blessings or positive occurrences in life and to meditate on them, so as to invoke peace of mind and raise the strength within me to deal with depressive symptoms.

When I realized the power of rejecting this ill proposed definition over my life, I saw a new hope to be someone bigger than my problems. Someone who would be bigger than my issues. I found some sort of strength to face future obstacles as I realized that if I had been through the worst, I could go through anything. Like gold refined in fire, we have the power to shine and develop unbreakable strength in our spirits before depression can have a chance to break us. We learn to self-regulate and to control our emotions through the experiences we go through which derive from the wisdom of making better choices in favor of self-satisfaction and happiness in our hearts.

You need to search your heart. You need to start searching yourself. The most important thing that you can use to motivate yourself to carry on in life is to identify that which gives you strength and builds your courage. Rejuvenate yourself through the strengths that you build in life. Cause your hopes and dreams to come true by setting your entire focus on achieving them. I realized that sometimes you need to do things outside of your comfort zone for you to identify what you are good at. I needed to push my limits and I attempted to do the things which I would not consider myself ever doing. When I began doing them, I felt a joy as what I had begun to do, caused me to develop immense confidence in myself to build experiences in different areas.

I felt as though I was in the process of gaining new knowledge and strengths. The more strengths I have, the more I can be pleased with myself about. The more I had to offer this world, the more hope I had in building a sustainable and hopeful future. I want to do great things one day and I know sooner or later that I would need to depend on the skills I have and build new ones, where needed.

Identify what you are good at. This has helped me to cope with the onslaught of negativity that depression builds. I know myself better in the present time and when those voices come to haunt me; that I am not sufficient enough to be apart of this world or to contribute greatly, I know how to reject them and move forward with my goal in mind.

When you have sought for the answers within yourself, you ought to fight back with the knowledge you have acquired. It is a battle that has endured in my mind for almost a decade now and I have experienced it in many shapes and forms, through different times in my life, and in different positions. It is a mental warfare. You fight for your right to be happy and for your sanity. You fight to be stronger and to develop the strength needed for future battles. I have developed the courage to fight back and to seek support where needed. Depression is something that can cripple you, but eventually you manage to pull yourself out of that trap and you will find the solution to your problems.

Remember this one thing, life will not afford you to confront what you cannot bear, but when you bear them, you will overcome. The answers will come to you as you make the effort to search. Keep your eyes open.

It all begins from the mind and from within.

4

THE MIND

"And to be renewed in the spirit of your minds...." – Ephesians 4:23

I

The human mind requires nurturing and reassurance whilst in duress or going through a stage of burnout. There is the power of positive thinking but sometimes we require a professional touch to help us out of our troubles. I want to discuss two forms of therapy which I have researched which assist in helping the human mind and improving the behaviour of individuals. It is vital to incorporate these facts to raise awareness about the specific aids which can assist the mind to restabilise.

In the practise of counselling and psychotherapy, there are notably a handful of therapeutic approaches and theories which are adopted by counsellors. These theories provide insight and knowledge into human behaviour, cognition and emotions. Behaviour therapy focuses on observed behaviour, learning experiences that influence individuals and has been used to treat many psychological disorders. This approach has also been used in all different kinds of areas to assist clients to treat mental illnesses. Existential therapy is an attitude of psychotherapy and is referred more specifically as a philosophical approach. It focuses on human themes such as life, meaning, death and other themes that influence a person's struggle. This approach can be used to assist clients to ponder upon their own lives and its meaning and reflect on how they can make life more meaningful.

II

Behaviour therapy originated within the 1950s and is based on the idea that all behaviour, either correct or wrong, is learned and can be influenced through conditioning. The original concept of this therapy came from the work of Ivan Pavlov, a Russian Psychologist, who had published a lot of studies on the conditioning system in the early 1920s.

The key concepts surrounding this therapy begins with views regarding human nature and this entails a methodological tactic for counselling. The notion of operant condition and classical conditioning are the two main concepts. Classical conditioning is used in behavioural training in which a neutral stimulus is paired with a naturally occurring stimulus and adopts the same response as the naturally occurring stimulus. Learning through association works by developing an association between an environmental stimulus and a naturally occurring stimulus and prominence of the stimuli and its timing play an important role in how quickly an association is formed. Extinction occurs when an association disappears which causes causing the behaviour to weaken gradually or vanish. Operant conditioning occurs through reinforcements and punishments and association is made between a behaviour and a consequence. Continuous reinforcement rewards all types of behaviour and is effective at the beginning of the operant conditioning process. Partial reinforcement involves offering a reward after several responses or after a period has elapsed. It is assumed that behaviours can be changed without delving too much into the origins of the psychological issues.

III

Existential therapy originated within the 1940s and the 1950s in Europe. This theory was influenced by key philosophical figures and writers in the 19th century about the existential issues of being alone and not having meaning in life, this therapy developed into what it is today.

The key concepts which give this theory meaning are empathy, positive regard and congruence. Empathy is a vital part which allows for the therapist to examine and feel the struggles of a client by adopting their viewpoint and in doing so, allows for an effective treatment, however, it only captures a range of the clients' views. Positive regard is the way therapist approach their clients in the sense of feelings and thoughts, and in turn can bring about changes in the client. This can influence success in the therapy if the therapist shares their positive views on the client with them and allow the client to understand their self-worth and evolve their ego.

Congruence is also known as genuineness, in which both the client and the therapist are truthful and transparent with each other. Congruence is a form of a person-centred therapy. For this to be successful in counselling, both the therapist and the client must work together in being truthful and thus the best result can be achieved.

IV

The therapeutic goals of behaviour therapy are to treat behavioural issues and psychological disorders in clients such as autism, drinking problems, anxiety and bipolar disorders. Behavioural therapy focuses on the main problem and involves the client to act for themselves and it can also be useful for treating issues like anger management and stress management.

The relationship between the therapist and their clients is seen to be critical to their clients' end goals. It is vital that this relationship involves the notions of warmth, empathy and authenticity and to establish a strong working relationship to meet their goals. For their goals to be effective, it is necessary for therapists and clients to establish first a meaningful relationship above all else.

The therapist's role is to firstly conduct an assessment on the client to identify any behavioural issues and to adopt the ABC model, which is to gather information on situational antecedents, then to identify the dimensions of the behavioural issues and to acknowledge the consequences of the client's wrong behaviours. This model is useful to identify what influences the clients' behaviours and the consequences of such behaviours. The therapist will also conduct a behavioural assessment interview which will assist in looking at specific antecedents and consequences which influence the behaviours that need treatment. Empirical evidence is crucial for the therapist as they tend to act as problem solvers for the clients.

V

The therapeutic goals of existential therapy are to overall, assist clients in finding meaning in their life and this form of therapy helps the clients to make the right and authentic choices to reach their full potential in life. Clients will discover what is true and remove false images on their life and themselves. Clients are assisted in taking responsibility for their life and acting to make the appropriate changes. This therapy will help clients become transparent to themselves challenge clients to be responsible over their lives and living fully daily.

The therapeutic relationship between the therapist and the client is vital for them to successfully be a helping hand by assisting the clients to take full control of their lives and decisions by engaging them in methods to take responsibility. The therapist must respect the client's views on themselves and work with them as they are both on a journey of self-discovery.

The function of the therapist is to challenge the aspects of their clients who shy away from responsibilities in life. The therapist also has the role of engaging clients by allowing the clients to question themselves in the situations they experience, based on what they have contributed to the situation. The therapist will allow clients to confront themselves and seek methods of self-reflection, based on their choices and responsibilities in life. This is essential for self-discovery and growth.

VI

The main techniques and procedures for behaviour therapy involve the operant conditioning techniques. Within operant conditioning specific behaviours are reinforced either positively or negatively. Positive reinforcement occurs when something rewarding is being added to certain behaviours whereas negative reinforcement is avoiding certain stimuli to improve behaviour. Behaviour is also manipulated through punishment, both positively and negatively. Positive punishment involves adding a stimulus consequently; therefore, causing the behaviour to cease. Negative punishment involves removing a reinforcing stimulus, consequently decreasing the behaviour. Classical conditioning is utilised for behavioural training and it introduces learning through association; which involves developing an association between environmental and natural stimuli. Systematic desensitization is a form of classical condition and exposure therapy that requires clients to expose themselves to anxiety arousing situations;

which helps them to confront and desensitize themselves to the stimuli. The strengths of this therapy are that it enables researchers to clearly observe and analyse behaviour over a period. It is effective for measuring and collecting data when researching, therefore, making it easier to change behaviours. This approach is scientific and it helps to replicate results. The overall idea of this therapy can be applied across various areas in real life; such as parenting, education and child care. The limitations are that the theories do not account for the free will of the unconscious mind and internal factors which influence results, such as clients' thoughts and emotions. This therapy neglects the cognitive side of the human mind which plays a vital role in influencing behaviours, therefore, not achieving accuracy when diagnosing.

VII

The main techniques and procedures for existential therapy involve adopting techniques from other therapies but usually revolves around understanding the subjective world of the client. The various methods used by these therapists derive from philosophical roots and views on human life and existence. Clients start off by understanding their own assumptions of the world around them and to clearly acknowledge the way in which they perceive the world and how they make sense of their reality. The therapist strives to help clients understand how they can take responsibility for their own actions in their own situations. Clients are then enabled to see their values and how much their own moral compass drives them. This revolves around self-exploration and clients can identify new values and adopt different attitudes to life. Finally, clients take what they have learnt newly about themselves and the therapist helps them to put it into action so that they may change the way they view their lives. The strengths involve assisting clients to discover meaning in their lives, even when they have negative views about the world around them and helps them to take more responsibility. Being a form of person-centred therapy, this allows the therapist to treat the client with respect and relation, which helps the clients to be related to and helps them to achieve the best result. There has been criticism that this form of therapy is atheistic, therefore people of different faiths do not feel comfortable in engaging. Therapists asks the individual to think about the larger aspects of life, such as the purpose of humanity, which can be conflicting for some individuals, who believe that their religions or faiths are responsible for answering these questions.

VIII

The preferable therapeutic approach would be existential therapy as it enables clients to achieve a new attitude and a new vision about their lives. This in turn can account for better life choices, including behaviour, and causing people to reach their full potential in life. The existential approach is seen to be as highly beneficial especially when applied to a vast multicultural context due to its broad perspective. Existential therapy shows that this theory is more open to various audiences and targeted to a wider range of people. The concepts involved also are especially effective in the sense that they are person centred concepts and they are most relatable to clients. In some cases, however, behavioural therapy would be effective, especially for those who suffer from behavioural issues. Studies have shown that roughly 75 percent of people who participate in behavioural therapy experience benefits from treatment. Behaviour therapy is best used for those who suffer from a lack of self-behaviour management and social skills. It is also most useful in a group setting and for intervention processes. Group leaders, based on the empirical data collected, can model and instruct ideal behaviour patterns which also gives a sense of accountability to all clients involved and this has mutual benefits for those involved in the collaboration.

Overall, both therapeutic approaches have various benefits and limitations and different methods for improving clients' wellbeing, but are both beneficial in their own specific setting and audience range.

IX

There are multiple benefits for the implementation of therapy but in some cases, the use of medication is recommended. With the help of chemical assistance and behavioural training, many people seem to recover and improve their mental state. However, does this totally wipe away the negative state of mind? People experiment different forms of anti-depressants and therapeutic approaches to identify which best suits their way of life.

The human mind consists of patterns in the way that it processes thoughts and people attempt to identify negative thoughts so that they may apply counter thoughts to improve their thinking. These methods are taught through therapy and counselling. While that is all well and good, it does not wipe away negativity forever. People must not become complacent that they lose guard of their minds and must always be aware of what they are feeding their minds.

It is noted that people can fully recover and come out from the clutches of mental illness, but whilst we reside in a negative world, we are still susceptible to falling back into the pit from which we struggled so hard to climb out of. We are to guard our hearts and our minds because whatever we think of ourselves; we become.

I have dealt with negative thoughts and they have plagued me for ten years. I have not fully recovered as my mind is constantly plagued with this but I am learning to live with it through strategies which I have learnt and proactively implement. My mind is very active and I need to stay one step ahead of it to ensure that I do not fall into a negative thought pattern. For once I am in it, it becomes difficult to come out of it.

The strategies I utilise involve accounting for the current blessings in my life. All of us have something which keeps us going: something that gives us a sense of purpose. I continuously look for something that can keep me going, whether it be accounting for the friends I have or the good accomplishments which I have received.

The power of the mind is underestimated and we must be careful of what we manifest into existence through our thoughts. The power of the mind is fuelled by what you perceive and what you think. Henceforth, it is encouraged that one comprises this with positivity and positive aspirations so that they may strive to achieve the best results.

I have formed images in an out of my mind and it becomes difficult to conjure positive thoughts when I am confronted with negative images. I need to acknowledge what I am conjuring and change it to positive images, which gives me reasons to believe in the power that can change your entire perspective.

X

It is the little things that give us joy. Happiness can be formed within our thought processes, based on our perspective of the world. We can create this happiness through the little things which most people take for granted or do not consider having considerable joy and value.

We bear witness to the events that go on throughout our daily life but do not stop to think whether they are beneficial to us if we were to be part of it. Instead, we look for the happiness that the world tells us to look for. We are brought up with the ideals of the world which shape our minds from the very beginning and we are in the pursuit of what the world wants us to pursue. We end up hollowed out due to not achieving the status that we have been told to strive for and then contemplate whether it was even the right thing to do. We only realize the issue in this when we start to question ourselves and the path.

This occurs in most people's lives and it's a habit formed by our upbringing in this world. The real happiness which we strive to seek comes from what we make out of the events which occur to us. When we stop and analyse situations in which we encounter and then count our blessings or observe how many benefits we are dealt, then we know the true value of what we have.

Most of us long for the feeling of being included and having a vast social circle. We long for people to acknowledge our existence with utmost attention and priority but the world does not work like that unless you sell out to a bigger organization which attempts to control your life. Yet, we do not consider the select few who would look after us in our times of trouble. What do people consider to be joyous? Having a big social circle in which you are in the limelight? OR considering the select few friends that you may have, that they would take a bullet or move mountains to ensure that you are well.

It is all inside our head and we have the power to change how we see things. The power of the mind is so great but it takes people their whole lives, through learning from experiences, to unlock the hidden potentials of the mind. We dictate our happiness through our desires, which in turn become our goals but our perceptions need to match up for us to be truly happy.

We must mentally visualise what we want for our lives and administer a construct for ourselves to perceive the path to true joy. When we dictate things for ourselves, we must be aware that we are not swayed by our surroundings and happenings which can easily provoke us to stray off the path.

The goal is to remain true to our joy, and improve ourselves through a positive mindset, with the help of professional methods, advice, ideals, achievable visions, etc. To keep life simple is key to greater joy.

5

FAITH

"Now faith is the assurance of things hoped for, the conviction of things not seen."- Hebrews 11:1

I

Over the course of my youth, I have grown up in and studied three religious faiths and beliefs and I have come to understand the different ideas and views that people have adopted towards the concept of life when involved in these religions. I was brought up in two religions before I had converted to Christianity. At present, I follow one way of life: Christianity, but before this I was sitting in the middle of the fence between Buddhism and Sikhism. I was born and raised as a Sikh originally and I began practicing Buddhism as well at a young age. In my teenage years, it appealed to me to explore the purpose and the hopes of life and what was in store of me. I needed to know what I was here to do and how I was going to do it. Was there anything specific? I needed to acquire hope and clarity of the questions of life and unveil the hidden meanings.

The various concepts in which I was studying had brought me a vast range of knowledge but I was always looking for something meaningful and special to me; which would fit into my heart perfectly. I longed for some sort of knowledge and affirmation which would fill gaping hole in my heart as I acknowledged that there was something in the spiritual side of me which was lacking. I managed to fill that hole to some extent, the moment I adopted Christianity and I have been a devout since.

My understanding of the various religions has given me a broad understanding of how people approach life. With the mindset of expecting different achievements and avoiding various consequences, everyone has adopted their own path to life and is driven by their religious or life values. People follow what they do out of fear of the higher power in their faith if they believe in some higher power, or if they do not, then by either family values or traditions set out before them in order for them to acquire lifelong happiness or purpose.

Speaking of religions, if you observe each faith carefully, there is a notion of reward at the end of one's life. To obtain that, one must be compliant to a certain set of commands or rules which the God(s) of their religion commands. The rewards consist of attaining a higher position with God in Heaven, or access to an eternal reaping of rewards. Their end goal, after death, is to dwell within a sovereign residence in the peaceful place of their Creator.

When people set these rewards before them, they alter their approach to life. They strive to achieve the promises made to them from the concept of their faith and they undertake the appropriate actions required of them to be true to their God. These people, in doing this, change their reality and alter their way of thinking. In some sense, they have created their own fantasy and have made it to be real because they have established a bridge between what they believe in and what they are living in.

II

People are always looking for something more. There must be some sort of meaning and explanation as to why we are here. What is the concept of the universe and what is the part of humans in it? Faith in a higher power which designed the universe has given people a sense of security and purpose in their way of life in wherever they reside and whatever they do.

The faith in which they believe in and the rules or commands that they revere drive the way they live and it brings them personal satisfaction when they successfully adhere to it.

People are convinced that the meaning of life resides in faith and religious practices and they adopt the practices that the religions propose. Faith is the fuel in the lives of most people which drives them to carry on and live out their days.

Faith can rewire an individual's state of mind through reshaping how the world works and their perspective towards everything. We have the basic understanding of the pattern or the world but each faith brings forth a specific set of instructions for the followers to abide by. Although some faiths intertwine and display similar traits, each one is unique to their believers and each one believes that their way is the ultimate way of life. However, not all people believe in a higher power, so they choose to have faith in things of the world.

I am sure you have heard the biblical expression "faith is believing without seeing". The meaning behind this is behind this I believe in God regardless of the fact that I cannot see Him with my eyes. I have to have faith that God is there and trust my experiences of His intangible presence. I see the meaning of this expression as to have hope in what you can't see happening, yet you visualise it manifesting. It could be something physical or it could be a situation that you are expecting. The idea is to hope for the best and if one believes in it strongly, whilst taking the best course of action to achieve it, it shall come to pass in time. This is the mystery of faith.

The biblical concept of faith explains it as an essence in which believers are required to believe and expect for things, whilst physically working things out to enable that which they believe in to occur. The bible says in 2 Corinthians 5:7 "For we walk by faith, not by sight." This concept can also be applied to modern life.

Other religious beliefs have a similar concept of faith, which is to believe in their creator for miracles to occur and for salvation. In their case, it is applicable to their lives as they acknowledge the power and potential of faith changing their lives.

III

"So that the tested genuineness of your faith—more precious than gold that perishes though it is tested by fire—may be found to result in praise and glory and honor...." – Proverbs 3:26

There has been many a time where my faith has been tested. I have felt the shadows of the darkness close around me as I was forced to behold the small ray of sunshine which came before me. As the light travelled forward, I had to press forward to receive it. The light which kept radiating at a minor rate was not being extinguished but seemed to grow larger and larger as I crossed the bridges of pain and pushed through the darkness which sought to engulf my soul. My being was forced to take hold of the light in hopes that it would extinguish the darkness. And lo, this is the journey of many to keep their eyes fixed upon the light. Maintaining resilience and never faltering, enduring to the end to obtain the rewards which have been prepared for us.

Greatness is built through adversity.

We hear stories of endurance and many tales of overcoming, but do we understand how people managed to come through? We assume to know what goes on in their situations but we can never comprehend their burdens until they are placed onto our shoulders. Then we are caught off guard and surprised by affliction.

We do not realize what could happen next and are left hopeless. In such cases, we ought to triumph by pressing forward. You will not be given what you cannot bear, but when you are challenged, there will be a way out. It is up to you to work out your own path and invoke the power of your faith, whatever it may be, to see you through your troubles.

The knowledge and understanding of making appropriate decisions to escape from your troubles comes only through experience. It is easier to inflict more hurt on your own life when you're passing through negative phases but it is not just about going through these things the easy way. Rather through hurt, you learn to deal with these things as you progress. It is all a learning curve. I had to endure and I hurt those around me, however, after making these mistakes, I learnt what NOT TO DO!! There is only so much one can teach you but in order to master life, you need to learn on the field.

IV

On this path of life, we must tread carefully, for there are many hidden snares. This is the authenticity of life. There are ups and downs in every path but we must adjust ourselves through vitality. We tend to sink low when we are complacent and there are multiple influences which shape us to be complacent.

Whether it be events or medical conditions, our mind will be subject to potential downfalls but it is our faith which carries us through. Multiple times throughout my army service I was brought down. Not just my army service but in life as well. At many points in my life, it felt as though every day was a struggle. An effort where being awake was not meant for me. I had to die.

We have to activate our faith to get ourselves out of the snare which entraps us. There are multiple snares but that is life. There will not always be a motivator and there will be times in which you will lack in determination. There will not always be a reason to keep pressing on but it is in the human mind to be resilient. It is an innate construct which forces us to see ourselves through.

Life can be filled with nothingness but our minds have the power to create something. Just through faith in ourselves or in a higher power will see us through our troubles. To each, their own in this choice of faith but something is better than nothing.

I had to utilize multiple motivators which were external until I had to find something within me which kept me going. I felt that I was never enough and that people never cared. What pushed me came from the inside as I thrived to achieve my dreams and aspirations. Sometimes you have to take it one day at a time.

As we can understand, faith is similar to hope and can also be the light in a dark place. It is the essence which can shift your state of mind from negative to positive. We know that hope is the optimistic expectation of something to happen. We all hold onto different types of hopes as we always expect something new to happen. Whether it be achieving a certain financial status or attributing your wealth to invest in a new house, there is always something or someone we hope to happen to us. We need new things to happen in life to engage our minds and to keep us thrilled to see what life can offer us next.

This is a journey of personal discovery which infuses our minds with excitement and revelation.

V

Understanding ourselves in this journey of faith and hope is a key element for us to receive what is purposed for our journey. We have to remain optimistic that good things will happen and that all events are somehow relatable to us for us to grow and mature within ourselves.

Everyone is allotted a specific portion of life experiences and events. Our attitude and approach towards our portions define what happens to us, what we experience and what we can expect to receive from it.

We receive good news with gladness but bear the bad news with sorrow. We have to accept both the good and bad with life. This is where we need to come to our senses, be mindful of what is happening in our lives and be prepared to deal with whatever cards we are dealt. Do not expect things to be so easy that you can cruise through it, but do not doubt yourself for a second because you can either allow it to bring you down or strengthen you mentally. We are defined through these struggles as the lessons we learn are the weapons we equip for our future battles.

Faith and hope allow us to maintain what we have received as we build confidence within ourselves to not shy away from challenges. We acknowledge that we have been through so much already, therefore whatever comes next, we will not budge but because we have kept our faith, we can persevere.

We must learn to let go of our pains when we have gone through experiences. There is a lot of mention about challenges but not enough about letting go of the baggage that we accumulated unwillingly. When we experience hurts, we tend to hold onto grievances towards people who have offended us or towards situations which have occurred. Situations have caused me to be bitter in my life but I had to encourage myself to let go of the pain and hope for the recovery, which indeed came in time. We cannot see the recovery ahead because we are too focused on the pains which hold us back. This is a cycle which needs to be broken and I encourage you to remove the hurts in your life. Forgive who or what you need to, let it go and have faith that all things will work together for your good.

VI

Forgiveness is a great power within you. It holds a spiritual, mental and physical benefit; should you choose to forgive. It is an act of realizing that you have been hurt, acknowledging who or what hurt you, making peace with it through pardon and CHOOSING to let go and move on from what hurt you. Choice is the key word here – forgiveness is a choice not something that can be forced against a person. Forgiveness is a sign of having faith because you choose to believe that something greater can and will result from this.

I have been betrayed many times in life. I have had people walk out on me and I have had people go against what I believed. I have lost meaningful friendships which have caused me deep regrets of not having done anything in my power to sustain these relationships. However, we must be aware that not everything is in our control and we must accept that.

People are far from permanent and will constantly enter and leave your life. Each person that enters your life will make an impact on your life before they leave; whether negative or positive. When the time comes for them to leave, you will not always understand. A counsellor had once told me that you do not always get to find out the reason behind why someone chose to leave the friendship, that you just had to accept it and let it go. When you make peace with it, you eventually stumble upon someone or something else that will make up for that void in your life. The way to save a lot of stress and heartache throughout the process is to forgive and let go. Manifest the best in all circumstances: friendships, relationships, job opportunities or educational doors. It is all about letting go and forgiving the situation. There is ample amount of time in life to forge new bridges of opportunity and there is never a limit to what you can have or do.

I tend to stumble in this quality at times but I have realized that this is a lifelong practice. You can never be good at this overnight. Although you might have the appropriate mindset to be ready to move on, your emotions can get the better of you at times and that is where the training needs to be applied. Emotions tend to foil what our mind sets out to do. We must incorporate logic and reason with a sound mind when deciding what to do next. We must look at the reality of things because the consequences that come with our choices are real and will definitely cause positive or negative effects. This is why I make multiple mentions of hoping for the best in all circumstances for with the power of hope and faith, one can strive forward and meet the next step in life. One can take hold of their next portion in life, with the acquired knowledge and realization that they can conquer anything that life throws at them.

VII

Self-reflection is a powerful tool that assists with self-discovery. It has similar traits to mindfulness but with reflection, you learn to break down your goals and ideas about life and can plan with specific targets and configure paths to take in meeting your visions.

Using self-reflection combined with having faith in what is to come can be an approach to a successful mindset. If you start to believe in what you have planned, you are already on the way to achieving it. Start off with faith in yourself, then determine the path you wish to take. You may not be able to see your goals and rewards as of yet but you should already visualize what you are going to achieve. Visualize yourself in that light of success, and hope to move in that direction. When you have faith, you can move mountains. Move those mountains in your life to create your paths in the direction you wish to go not simply the direction that has been set for you.

I have learnt in life that the power of faith abounds over pain when one puts all of their heart and soul into believing and hoping for the best. I always had doubts about myself and my journey in life. I never stopped to nurture my emotions and my thoughts, but when I began to practice being faithful to something, I learned that it is easier to shed worry and anxiety when one is hopeful of the things to come. In other words, learn to hope instead of worry.

The vigilance of what the mind is expecting is crucial to understanding how your personal faith can be worked out. Take time to sit down and reflect over what you believe in. Be mindful of what you stumble across in your ever flowing train of thoughts. It helps to associate your emotions with your aspirations and hopes for the future. The mind is key to improving yourself and making yourself to be the best version of you.

Do not hold doubts about your life but learn to realize that if you make the effort mentally, the physical results that would manifest in your life will be fruitful in your adventures.

6

ANIMA INQUISITION

I want to talk about soul searching. We as human beings desire to have a purpose and want immense joy and meaning in all that we do in life. there also has to be some reward for us to keep us energized and on the course of pursuing our desires. At times in life, anyone can feel stuck, lost, empty, alone or isolated. There is the temptation of wanting to end everything that you have you been doing or living for because there's a profound sense of dissatisfaction with everything. By everything, I talk about every aspect of life. Being stuck in this part of life can cause the following:

- You feel constantly lethargic and fatigued.
- You lose your motivation.
- You become uneasy with yourself
- You feel isolated
- There is unhappiness within yourself
- You are looking for that something ‹more› (This is something I have deeply resonated with recently and it has led me to write this.)
- You feel like you›re invisible to society.
- You latch onto anything that can stimulate your mind or give you a ‹rush›, whether it is good or bad for you.
- You want to numb the pain but nothing seems to work.
- You are broken.
- Depression takes over
- Mental health issues start to develop.
- There is a missing piece in you but you can›t identify it.
- You›re bored with everything.
- You lose yourself.

With all these prevailing negative traits and emotions, you succumb to sojourning in a realm where you feel emotionally detached from the world and lost in society. I have gone through these rough patches where I have felt I was lost and 'invisible' to society. I would stand and watch as everyone would pass by with some sort of resolution which enables them to function in society as purposeful human beings. At times, I feel like everyone around me has some meaning to their lives or something to do with their time, whilst I do not. I have adopted a coping mechanism which is to constantly keep busy with hopes that I would find some sort of meaning in the jobs I do, whether it be work related or educational.

The idea of soul searching has led me to question the meaning of myself. What is my soul worth? Is there something which my existence represents? What encompasses my path in life which would hopefully lead me to the discovery of myself? I decided that I needed to find some sort of meaning in myself and my soul.

I start with the search of my meaning in God and by doing good to others through service. Very simply put, God says that everyone, according to the Bible, has importance, purpose, meaning and an abundantly planned out life before them. The key is to tap into this secret by first seeking to search the truth of what the Creator has been teaching us according to his Scripture. The meaning of our souls has been warped as the world has progressed. The modern world only gives importance to the rich and famous. What about the rest of society? What about those who contribute to the world in the shadows who keep their identities a secret? The good works of people are not seen as important if they are not recognized, according to the laws of this world. However, the good you do for someone or a majority will be deemed important by the them, who will validate it, as it remains only between the two parties.

I follow the teaching of the Bible which tells us not to boast of the good works we do, rather to do them in secret and God shall reward them openly, that all may see them. This biblical concept encourages people to do good which is seen as important and justified by God himself. So why do you need people to validate the importance of your work when the Creator and all His angels are bearing witness to the goodness which you display. This is something that I have tried to understand so that I can be satisfied that what I do has importance in some sense and it gives my soul some value as well.

I still try to grasp that we have meaning in our existence but it gets more difficult as I go through each day. With the negativities of society, I find that on many occasions, I feel very invisible. I do not feel as though I am recognized and all I do counts for nothing. I really want my life to have some meaning and I want to pursue all the good in the world that I may be a part of it, so that I can reward myself with purpose and true joy. Doesn't everyone want happiness?

I did some soul searching in the midst of being alone. When you're alone in a place of solitude, you have little choice but to learn to live with your senses. This is a time where it is helpful to be mindful of the thoughts you inhibit whilst existing in the current place. Being mindful of yourself allows you to further explore your own mind and what you are contemplating at that time. It would pay to be weary that your mind does not wander off into negativity. It is an opportunity for you to discipline your mind to think of positivity and not to dwell on loneliness. You are not alone when you have your purpose and your meaning living with you. You can use this opportunity to express yourself freely and take heed of the areas in life that you need to work on and improve, or things that you want to do differently. This is an exceptional moment for self-discovery as you are in a state of contemplation with minimal worldly distractions. Envision yourself in a true state of serene bliss and then make use of it to set out a plan for what you want out of yourself in life and how you can go about fulfilling your dreams.

I tried to discover what my true emotions are by allowing my weaknesses to surface so that I could learn to be strong. Only when you are refined by fire do you develop a soul of iron. In life, you need to be able to identify your strengths and your weaknesses and use them to guide you to search for your purpose and meaning. As a person grows during their lifetime, events happen which catapult them into the deep end multiple times. It has happened to all of us. We are backed up against a wall with no choice but to push forward in order to overcome. This is how we learn to pull ourselves out of the messes in our life. Draw inspiration from people who have been through trials. Look for ways to carry on. I found that a lot of methods I used came to be naturally as I learned to do battle within my mind. The opportunities and methods to overcome will come to you, but you need to display the sheer will and determination to press on and not to give up. We are made to persevere.

Reflect on your life and visualize the road ahead of you. Are you content with the way you are travelling? Make the necessary changes or have a pit stop in the road of life. It does not hurt to adjust your path but ensure that it is all for the good of yourself and those around you. Build your dreams and envision them. See how you will accomplish them down the path and live for that. It will surely be used as your drive in life. So, use it!

Always remember, that what you seek is not always so far away. Most of the time, we do not realize that the answers can be found within us.

7

BE GOOD TO YOURSELF

"Surely goodness and mercy will follow me all the days of my life......" -Psalm 23:6

I

I am sure that you have heard somewhere in your life that you should be kind to yourself. That you should look after yourself and be good to yourself first before spreading that kindness to others. Well, I have to tell you that it is true and that you should abide by this where possible. Many people neglect themselves in this age because they are distracted by being something else. They notice the good things in others but have a hard time reflecting on their own goodness. They aspire to imitate others' images and dreams, whilst abandoning their own. What is the point in that when you end up losing yourself? You do not gain anything other than sorrow in trying to become something that you are not. You are born in a specific way with a special path and you should accept that. The soul that dwells within your body is especially created to contribute something special to the operation of this world and to bring gifts to the lives of others.

When you were created, there was a spark of light that entered the glumness of this world. When you began to walk, the world began to experience a new joy and the anticipation of a brand-new gift that would contribute to the society in which you were placed. When you began to learn, the world did not hide anything from you, but all the knowledge and mysteries of the universe began to reveal itself to you. The purposes instilled in your life, when you work them out, will unravel itself into the flow of the world. You will begin to realise your own persona within when you pay attention to your own needs. The method in which you do so is up to you, whether it be realization or an experience which triggers you to find yourself. When you acknowledge these things about yourself, you will erupt with confidence that you can do whatever you aspire to do.

The thrill of being unique is lacking in this world. In today's age, society engulfs the minds of individuals from a young age as they unwillingly conform to be the same as others. As though we are mindless robots, striving towards the shared purpose of a hive mind. This is not the case as each person was born to stand out. It can be very difficult to stand out, I get it. Nonetheless, it cannot hurt to try. There should be some sort of effort to create and image on yourself which sets you apart from the rest of the world. In being different, there is importance. People are afraid of being different due to the fear of persecution. They are afraid of being judged or laughed at. The wicked looks of society are paralysing enough for someone who is only trying to venture out with something new to show. Why is this the case? Each person's fingerprints and DNA are so unique and there is none other. Even identical twins have differences despite looking too similar to distinguish.

Society has not been kind to the latter generations and there is not enough encouragement to be different. Well, at some point or another you just might get sick of conforming and may decide to wake up to yourself. Realizing that it is alright to be different. Realizing that you have all the potential and energy to symbolize the uniqueness of your being. That is alright to be you.

Doing something different which causes you to stand out is special because you learn to go against the tide. You learn that in order to develop something special in yourself, you need to go the opposite way of the crowd, dare to dream big and establish a mindset of perseverance. I seek to stand out from the crowd on a daily basis and have resorted to brainstorm as many methods that would support me in doing so. I do not want to be like everyone else, I wish to rise my potential peak in life and perform to the best of my abilities daily. It started when I decided to discover my true meaning. The very reason for my existence is something I have sought out in numerous ways because I need that gratification in myself to keep going in life. The search for meaning will eventuate in all of us at some point of our lives. It might require a significant incident in our lives or a lesser event that will catapult us into the land of discovery and self-searching.

I want to know what I am made up of and what defines me. I want to know if it is worth being me, or whether I should change to be something more attractive to others; something more attractive to this world. I feel like I am not enough for this world. I have always felt out of place or that I am just not meant to fit in. I decided that I wanted to be something different enough to stand out that the world would eventually accept me.

You are special.

II

You should start off by loving yourself. Have you asked yourself what it is about you that can make you be set apart from others? We all have special paths in life. Although we might draw inspiration from individuals who have been famous or have accomplished something great in this world, the path we walk cannot be imitated perfectly by anyone else no matter how hard they tried. We need to make the rightful claim over our lives own it. Take responsibility over your actions, thoughts and feelings. Instruct yourself to be bold to go for opportunities and take positive risks, so that even if you do not achieve what you thought to do, you would have grasped some sort of lesson. The mind is built to expand and it expands based on what you feed it. Feed it with positivity and self-affirmations.

Learn your own habits and cull the habits that do not serve any purpose in you. When you act, think before you do. Determine, through self-evaluation, what course of action you should take to benefit your purpose and of those around you. When you do something, or make some choice, you cast a ripple across the ocean of this world. You affect someone or something somewhere, and it is your intention of that ripple which either benefits others or causes them to stumble. Take heed of advice on areas which you need to improve. Constructive feedback is never to bring you down but to build you up. Be open to the criticism you receive in this life and do not take it in a bad way. Use it to strengthen you in areas that you lack. Words can cause harm, as the tongue is the most powerful part of the body. You can either edify someone by the way you speak or bring them down. So be mindful of what you say. Your tongue, like your mind, has the power to manifest positivity in your life, so use it for the better.

I believe that the strongest of us has been through the deep waters. They have made a way for themselves and have made a way for others to swim through those treacherous waters of life. there is no need for dismay because you can choose to alter how well you swim in them. It is all in your hands, to carry out your life in bliss and harmony or to invite unnecessary struggle. You can start off by loving yourself especially because you serve a purpose. It is up to you to work it out and bring realization to yourself.

I believe in you. You are strong.

III

Spend time with yourself. Earlier on in my life, I had anxieties of being alone. I was always afraid of being lonely. I desired company no matter where I went or how I felt. I always desired some form of company and I depended on that religiously for comfort and confidence. I lacked the strength to be alone and it was severely daunting, perhaps because I never had people spend time with me constantly, yet I felt that I needed it. I depended too much on the company of others that when I was alone, even for an hour, I began to sink into the train of my thoughts which engulfed me in loneliness.

I never saw the value of spending time with myself. I never built the courage to accept that at many points in life, I would have to do things by myself or spend days at a time without much contact from the world. I had to get used to the comfort of my own shell when I realized the reality of life. You are going to feel lonely at times. You won't be able to help being without the company of those who you desire. Life carries everyone in its own path and for some seasons, your path and that of others may not cross for some time. So, what are you going to do about that? Are you going to allow the loneliness to invite itself in and cradle you in its dark bosom, where you feel hopeless and depressed because you feel as though the world has shut you out?

You do not have to do or feel just that. I felt it many times over especially when I was in Singapore for my army service.

I felt it the most because I felt foreign to the nation. Everyone I met had grown up there and had a secured connection with their own friends and family. I knew that I wasn't the only one who felt this way, yet I could not shake off the negativity that it brought. During the two years, I had moments where I felt the loneliest. Still, I think to this day that it was the worst time.

Whilst my friends and immediate family were back home in Melbourne, I felt I was a world away, in a distant land far from everything, metaphorically speaking. That was what my mind conjured up anyways. I had to sit through it and I could never manage to make myself feel better unless I spoke to someone about it. I needed constant reminders that people were there for me. The anxiety of it really took a hold of me and brought me to my lowest.

I began to feel like a burden upon people, as I was constantly seeking for reassurance. This resulted in me having to teach myself how to cope. It was in this state where my mind taught me how to affirm myself. Affirmations, which is a sense of emotional support, edify your own soul especially when it comes for yourself. It is effective to administer this in self-care. You'll find that you will affirm yourself many times in life, almost daily, in order to keep yourself going. Affirmations can come in different forms and from various sources. It is as simple from telling yourself that everything is going to be alright to having people lend a shoulder to cry.

When there are no people in reach, that is when it becomes difficult to rely on others. That is what I experienced and therefore I had to lean on my own shoulder. The affirmations I had to produce for myself were challenged by my own mind. I produced a lot of self-doubt and whenever I believed something positive about myself, my mind would counter that with demeaning and doubtful thoughts.

The only way I honestly overcame this was by pushing doubt out of my mind and having faith and what I said. I forced myself to believe the positive affirmations about myself and did so till it became so easy for me to be positive about myself and I would not hold any doubts about it. It is a process easier said than done but it has proved to be fruitful over time.

It is fascinating that when even you are going through something, the mind can be both your enemy and your friend. Your mind can create something to support you but it needs to have an external stimulus for it to be engaged and to create something positive for yourself. This is why it is vital to spend time and be mindful of what is happening in your life to identify what can be received as good.

Another method I adopted was to manifest my blessings into a written format to serve as reminders for whenever I needed motivation. I felt that feeding my mind with a physical positive stimulus would encourage my mind to expand in the creation of more positivity for myself. Whenever the doubts would come, I would retreat to my written list of blessings and would meditate on them. I became mindful of what I had written and committed them to memory if I needed the blessing list on the go.

Powerful reminders serve as effective motivators because when you write it down, you can convince your mind to combat doubt and believe in the truth that you have written. And you will know if it's true by the way you sense that piece of information through your emotions and by utilizing logic. Ask yourself of the blessings in your life and know it to be true. Whatever is true, make note of it. Do not lie to yourself. You never know that even your written blessings can contribute to changing aspects of your life.

I know that it changed mine because I felt that my state of mind was evolving and I learned to better control my emotions. I learned to block out doubts about myself and could identify the lies which was being fed to my soul.

IV

"Having gifts that differ according to the grace given to us, let us use them..." – Romans 12:6

Each and every person that has entered into the cycle of this world has been imparted into them a certain set of qualities and gifts which define them especially and sets them apart from the rest of the human race. Each individual holds a significant value and bear special treasures in their heart, which determine the path of their life. Their cultures and beliefs pave the path of their life but the gifts which they possess determine how and where they can contribute to society or be a part of a greater scheme and picture.

When you have discovered and in turn determined the unique skillset which you possess, it can help you to see the value in your life. You begin to understand your self -worth and can envision the course of your future. Where you apply your gifts brings forth outcomes, either good or bad, but it is up to you to decide; keeping in mind that you will reap what you sow. In other words, what goes around comes around.

People usually identify their skills and gifts and use it to plot the course of their life in their educational path or careers. Take this opportunity to identify your own gifts. Determine what makes you feel good about yourself and what you use to carry yourself across the seas of life. Determine what you about yourself can be used to help others through their problems. It can be easy to identify at a young age, whereas, others are required to go through certain troubles or circumstances in their life to see what is born from their struggles.

You can literally be the hero of your life or the hero of others'. People will appreciate what you can pull out of the treasure box of your heart. They will be proud of how you develop them. When you persevere in troubles, your gifts will be fashioned and trained to be used for even greater circumstances. You can be part of something bigger than yourself if you just decide within yourself; that yes, I am going to see what my gifts are and use them, in any way, to provide help and spread joy to others.

You can fill so fulfilled when others enjoy what you have. Others may be envious of you but that is not the point. From what you have learnt about yourself, share with others to identify their own gifts. The appreciation will go far and they will remember your name.

V
___

"Whoever has a bountiful eye will be blessed,
for he shares his bread with the poor."- Proverbs
22:9

Dream big and see the world: you might learn something about yourself and the world. I learned to appreciate what I had when I went to India at the end of 2019. It was my first time in India. I visited Chennai and Tirupati. I discovered a simple way of life and with it the hardships of those less fortunate. I saw many homeless people walking about. Whatever their circumstances were, I did not know but I felt something in my heart move, as though I wanted to do something. I wondered how much I could do for so many people when I was by myself.

I recounted all the times I took my circumstances for granted. This is part of what inspired this book: being grateful for what you have and in turn, change your way of thinking. The homeless always had a special place in my heart. If only I could snap my fingers and solve the homeless problem in this world. Sadly, it does not work like that.

I saw beggars roaming about with bags. I saw people living in houses that looked like they were built hundreds of years ago. People had no electricity. They showered from a pail. I saw that they did not have access to the luxuries that I have access to. I realized what it meant to take things for granted. I took everything I had for granted.

Seeing this made me realize how privileged I was. We cannot help everyone in the world but if we can do our best and make an attempt to change one person's life, it would make all the difference to them. I realized that in order to grow, one method of doing so is to see what hides on the other side of the planet. To wonder what life is like for others who are affected by lesser circumstances and then to see it for real, changed my perspective on how I view life.

It is most effective when you see everything for real. When you share the same space and air as those who are affected by sickness, poverty, etc. I saw that those people were living a simple way of life. With simple technologies and labors, I saw the will of them to live and carry on despite their lack of luxury. It is truly a mystery to which I am still trying to figure out.

What I took away from it was to be grateful for what I have, and that having a heart for these people, to use my gifts to cater to the needs of the impoverished. When you see with your eyes, something in your soul will move, something in your heart will be triggered. Use it, I say. Use that in you for the betterment of mankind. Be good to yourself and look after yourself, so that when you do so, you may look after others. That is what I believe in my heart is the true purpose of life.

"Whoever brings blessings will be enriched, and one who waters others, will himself be watered."-
Proverbs 11:25

8

LIGHT AND ENERGY

"The light shines in the darkness, and the darkness has not overcome it."- John 1:5

I

I was granted the opportunity to be a light in the darkness whilst I was in the army. It was during a ceremony where we received our rifles. Our rifles: the Singapore Assault Rifle- 21, symbolized our tool for the defence of a proud nation. It was now when I first held a rifle that I could sense a great burst of pride rising in me. I slightly shed tears as my commanding sergeant major put his hand on my shoulder in approval of my conviction as a soldier. For the first time in my life, I felt I was put on this earth for a purpose. I sensed that I was put on this planet to be a defender and that through my soldiering, I would be a fortress for the people of Singapore. I was trained with the purpose to combat the opposition, should any arise, both physically and mentally. I was determined to put all that I had into this defence training and was greatly convicted in the ideals and purpose of being a solider. After receiving our rifles, we began training with it. We learnt to take care of it and to holster it with pride. I felt powerful with my weapon. It became a part of me as I utilized it in our range life fire exercises and I never thought that I could have been a skilled marksman. My rifle training allowed me to feel like a protector. Although a weapon is an essential tool, I realized that through continuous training and safe handling, that the man behind the weapon instils it with capability and efficiency. This was the true source of my power; me!

Over the course of my life, on several occasions I have felt the need to be a protector. I desired possessing the characteristic of being someone who would combat the darkness and to be a protector of some sort. I desired the power and equipment which would give me the authority to execute my role as a protector swiftly. This longingness has been placed in my heart since I joined the army and I have learned to understand what it means to be a flicker in the world of darkness.

The light outshines the darkness no matter what the circumstance. Darkness cannot engulf the light because the light was created to oppose it. The sun is greater than the moon and so are you against all that would oppose you. We were created in the essence of light and based on our free will, we can choose to work with the light or be a part of the darkness. The source of the light has adapted through-out the years, from ancient religions and civilizations, to modern entertainment, cinema and acts of valor in civil defense, etc.

When you think of light, you might instantly imagine something pure, something that is holy, with great radiance which brings forth serenity and pure joy. All that is good in this universe is brought forth from the essence of light. The universe was created from light.

God said; *«light be, and there was light. And God saw it, that it was good...»- Genesis 1:3-4.*

When we adopt the light alone it is not sufficient. We must formulate the light in us. Every action of kindness, every thought of goodwill, is an example of letting our light shine. We are beings made for good, yet the darkness in the world perverts us and we become lost in the threshold of worldly lusts. The lusts of the world and the darkness therein, will fade away but our actions determine the legacy we leave behind. Are we a vessel of light and do we radiate good energy? Or are we a part of the perversion of this world which has dominated mankind from the beginning of time? We are living beings with a soul and a spirit, we generate an energy or supposed 'aura' around us. People can literally feel it.

As humans, we naturally sense the vibes of others around us. Our sensations and perceptions usually due do not mislead us. For example, if you have a 'gut feeling' about some place or something, it is often true. We can pick up the vibes of the people around us and it can assist us in determining their personality and what they intend towards us or others. The events and the environment in which they occur give us vibes and we perceive whether we are comfortable to remain in it, or move on elsewhere to seek comfort.

In this same sense of speaking, we as humans give out vibes and that can determine the company we attract. If we wish to be amongst likeminded people, we must provide the appropriate vibes which suit our personality. These frequencies are usually involuntary; which means that even if we do not realize or intend to, our being is always sending out these messages to attract our desires or something unexpected. We can alter these frequencies within ourselves by generating our mind with positive thoughts and intentions. When we do so, we can better practice what we give out and then can expect the same in return. Whether we choose to be kind or friendly to a loner, it reflects our energy output into our environment. We can then in return expect similar occurrences for ourselves later down the track. This is just a simple explanation for "what goes around, comes around", in a practical sense, so to speak. I do not claim full knowledge of how it all works but based on experiences which I have encountered, I am satisfied in this rough explanation.

II

Think what you will, speak what you desire. Do you comprehend the power of positive thinking? I used to be so negative in my youth, and sometimes still am, but only until I determined the power of thinking positively and speaking positive occurrences out into manifestation by faith. Simply visualize what you want to happen, ensure that it is for your good and for the good of others around you, speak it forth, and of course; you need to work it out physically. There is no magic to it. You need to speak it out and aim towards achieving it. Even when you are in the darkest trials of your life, it is up to you to define your outcome and work it out for yourself. You need to practice self-care, learn to pull yourself out with the power within you. We were made to persevere and if you can adjust your mind with this positive outlook, you might just finish the race set before you.

Setting goals and dreaming of the things you wish to accomplish is a major key in finding yourself. As you plan your life, you envision the details of the steps you ought to take. Being ambitious can propel you to great lengths as you set it in your mind and heart to follow the road to success. The visions come first, then comes the hard work to get there. Time flies really fast when you stay committed to a cause.

Whatever you decide to do in your life, finding yourself should be one of those things on your priority list. I am still looking for myself as I remember that this is a task to which I shall eventually complete. Do the things you love and attempt to do things out of your boundaries. Sometimes, the things that happen to us in life show us what we are made of and those qualities contribute to who we are.

As human beings, we are always developing in interests and dislikes. We can change our minds almost daily about almost anything. Finding yourself is something that can take a long time and there is no definite answer as to who you are really, but the answer that you give yourself by what you choose to experience and block out.

This is your life and the power is in you. Go out there and use what you have to create a deeper meaning of your life.

I was probably the most negative person in the world at one point of my life. When I first became depressed, I felt I was thrown into the deep end in my life. I did not know how to manage it nor what to do to help myself. I saw multiple psychologists who could only offer me self-help tips but what I discovered about how to deal with myself, I had to learn it myself. Not discrediting counsellors, psychologists or mental health workers, but sometimes you need to work it out yourself. When you manage to pull yourself up a little bit, you begin to realize that you have the innate knowledge which has been activated during your troubles, for you to endure and push forward.

I proposed that I was a lost cause and I was doomed to go through this for the rest of my life. I could not look beyond the horizon and see any hope for myself. I felt I was stuck in an endless quicksand of grief which constantly pulled me down. The vast range of suicidal thoughts haunted me and they came in every variation and situations. They would not leave me alone. In hindsight, the energy I must have produced must have been like an odor which lurked around me and would not dissipate no matter how hard I tried. I tried to make people smile as much as I could in hopes that I would feel better. Through my sorrows I made the utmost effort to be nice to people and to always help anyone I could, but I suppose the phase I was going through had to play itself out and yet I realize now that I was beginning to learn valuable life lessons which could be used in practice for the improvement of the mindset.

III

The brain does not fully develop for men until the age of twenty-five. I did not think it was fair for me to go through the lowest point in my life at the age of fourteen, but I could not choose what was written into my path. I simply had to bear my burdens. Something else I did to try to lift my spirits was to make as many friends as possible and offered to be there for them. I wanted to be known as the nicest person and someone that people could approach for advice and help. In high school, unless you were an introvert, it was not hard to acquire valuable friendships. I did not lack in having friends, yet in the crowd, I felt the most alone. Probably because no one understood what I was going through. Although no one understood me, I willed that none should be going through what I went through. Without fail, I always offered a hand to my peers. I did not realize that in the long run I was helping myself because now, I understand that I was preparing and training myself to help others later in life. When I felt the appreciation of the peers I sought to help, I felt temporarily whole and the happiness would suffice for a short amount of time. I needed something that was long term. Sounding like a drug, happiness was the only thing I craved and was willing to do whatever it took to achieve it. The idea of reaching happiness was so enticing but I was wrong to think that it was an end goal. Happiness in fact is a state of mind, much like other things and that happiness is a journey which must be worked out daily. It is an emotion and perspective which needs to be chosen daily above other things. To radiate positivity, one must be satisfied within themselves.

People stumble at various stages in their life and they require mature guidance to navigate their path and to work themselves out. People at a young age usually tend to have a higher chance of making a mess of their lives. Just because I finished high school at the age of eighteen, I thought that I was a knowledgeable adult. Filled with adrenaline and excessive energy, I ran towards adult life thinking I knew it all and had all the knowledge in the back of my head. How wrong I was. There was no way I felt so confident without being egotistic. I did not realize that I could make such a mess of myself at a young age and with my pride hurt, I deemed life was all about how you live and you learn. I pursued after wrong relationships in life and made efforts with the wrong people. I thought I knew the outcomes of every choice I made but in fact I was making mistakes. The things I chose for myself would come back around to hurt me. There were adults to guide me, but it was the choice I made of not heeding advice. I should have made more effort in the army, I should not have dated some girls, I should have kept some friendships closer or not said the wrong thing at the wrong time. In my juvenile state of mind, I believed I was doing the right thing but every time something broke down, I realized what NOT to do. I realized that I should have heeded the warnings of my elders and made certain choices instead of what I did. It is so important to have adult guidance i.e. – parents and mentors. I should have listened to everything my parents said instead of dismissing their advice. Older people have been through various experiences in life and they have done most of the things young people are thinking of doing or done at present. They have acquired more knowledge and made their share of mistakes, so that now they can pass on their knowledge to the younger generation. Take it from me, when older people advise you, take it and treasure it. They are attempting to pass their knowledge onto the younger generation. Make the right choice and do not cause those who care for you unnecessary grief. Take it from me, when older people advise you, take it and treasure it. Make the right choice and do not cause those who care for you unnecessary grief. Most of all, do not cause yourself unnecessary grief. You would rather spend on that time enjoying yourself and making the most out of your limited life. However, even though I am saying this, it may be something people might need to experience to learn from. If people never listened but still worked things out, then it is alright, because after all we are humans. Making mistakes due to stubbornness is sewn into our personalities from the start.

Learn to turn darkness into good. Easier said than done, but with practice you learn how to better deal with your unfavorable experiences. When you come across a problem, learn to change it for good so that you can deal with the problem easier. I have incorporated mindful thinking when I meet with problems and this helps me to deal with it easier through acceptance and peacemaking, rather than overthinking and panicking about it. I accept that I must deal with something and start off by cutting off any anxiety that I have. I change my negative thoughts into positive thoughts, i.e.- Visualizing a situation as vastly challenging or looking at it from the perspective it will make me stronger in the long run. I accept any situation which encourages me to challenge myself and in turn, construct opportunities to find a way out of it. Even relying on supports such as friends and family help me to deal with my situations. Do not panic, everything has a solution and if you see it that way, life will be easier.

IV

Often, sensing something supernatural or the energy of a location began to trigger me to ponder on the realms that coincide with the physical. The supernatural realm has been real to me as I have sensed things that cannot be explained without thorough examination or studying the situation scientifically. People fear what they do not understand but as you study faith and religion, you automatically become aware of the spiritual side of things. This is where you begin to detect forms of energy and start to question the supernatural. I have come across these situations, especially during my army service, where I felt uneasy in my army barracks. My fellow soldiers would describe sensing similar things and they said it was 'haunted'. I woke up one night and went to the bathroom and I felt that someone was behind me as I was at the urinal. The hairs on the back of my neck began to stand. And when I washed my hands at the sink, I felt yet again that something was directly behind me. During the night, my bunk mates would share that they had seen something strange during the night or would feel an unexplainable presence in the bunk with them. Although I was sound asleep, they said they heard noises, banging, and scarping of sharp objects across the metal surfaces of our lockers in the night. We never saw anything physical but we could sense things we could not explain. Now

I am sure that there is something psychological and scientific behind these sensations. Perhaps our senses were heightened during the silence of the dark night, but sure it was too much of a coincidence if many of us encountered the same thing. This is a description of an example of a darkness I sensed at one time and maybe because I believe in these things too much, that I began to manifest them unwillingly. Was this real energy or imagination?

I have sensed an exceptional peace in a church which I attended once which I could not describe it in words. The peace felt almost heavenly, with a soothing bliss. Once again, I believe in such things, so was I manifesting them unwillingly in my mind? I cannot stress how peaceful it was. It was as though heaven had opened and pierced the atmosphere of the church and us worshippers had received God's touch. It left me relaxed and forgetting about the troubles of the world. This is not something I saw with my eyes, but I was convinced in my heart of the peace because my senses were overwhelmed with calm. One by one, other worshippers claimed to feel some blanket of peace and began to praise God for it. So, I was not the only one who felt some sort of energy, like in the army barracks. The presence of God which orated through His Peace had caught us off guard and left us wondering if it was truly the touch of Heaven. Was this real energy or imagination?

V

In this world, there will always be light and darkness. The war between good energy and dark energy will rage on in an eternal battlefield. We as humans are caught in no man's land

and it is our choice to step onto whichever side we choose. It is up to us to determine which path our life is going to take. Although not all of us are given the choice, we can still make changes to our path when we learn to manipulate how we deal with our issues and strengthen our mindset. There is a very real spiritual side to life on earth and there are hidden powers working in our midst. This is the reality of it, and should you choose not to believe, you will eventually see or feel it.

Do not be afraid of stumbling or being caught up in the bad side of life, for this is where to begin to learn your own strengths and weaknesses. You get to experience the energies which work around you daily and the energy within yourself as well. Whatever influence we give into; we should correlate with the energy we wish to radiate. Ensure that it benefits you in the long run. Be in your area of peace and ensure that you reap the best of things wherever you choose to be.

> *"The night is far gone; the day is at hand. So then let us cast off the works of darkness and put on the armor of light." – Romans 13:12.*

9

CONQUER AND EXPAND

"...In all these things we are more than conquerors..."- Romans 8:37

I

Expand your experiences and you will conquer yourself and your boundaries. The planet we inhabit is teeming with experiences, culture, histories and wonder. From the far corners of the earth to the center of the equator, people from all walks of life radiate with vast cultures and traditions. The nations of the world are spread across a meridional circumference of 40,008 km, hosting 195 countries. Could you not explore and be enriched with enough experiences in a lifetime? The human race has adopted a whole heap of ideals and knowledge which has been spread to all corners of the Earth. What was once lost, is continuing to be found and the spoils of the hidden treasures are distributed amongst the peoples of the Earth. The mysteries and wonders of the Earth are sufficient to satisfy the generations yet to come for the sake of exploration. The advanced technologies which cater to humans vastly outnumber the provisions given to utilize them, yet humans have a constant hunger of knowing more and seeking what comes after the horizon. The world continues to develop across all the vast continents, emerging with different technologies and products which are physical, biological, technological, etc. The richer nations fill the lesser nations with awe and vice versa, in the sense of either geological or man-made constructs.

There are so many things to reach out to as our race expands with creation. Every day, there is something new to experience and something new to see. So why do we remain dormant in our own niches? Why do we not set aside expenses to set out and explore the world? What in our minds is stopping us from stepping out? And there are those who are longing for a full life. Those who come under the poverty line and those who are ill-stuck. Fighting to live another day and fighting for their next breath. From the corridors of the hospitals, those in palliative care begin to think of their whole lives. What have they amounted to? Are they satisfied with what they have done or do they continuously envision what they could have done different? What they could have seen or experienced to add to their book of adventures. Is there all there is to life or is there more? I wonder how many are satisfied with simplicity and how many put their explorer boots on daily; ready to be refreshed with something new.

II

I always find myself asking "Is that it?!". Whilst we are young and strong, sturdy and able-bodied, we should seek to explore what is new and what is to come. Our state of mind tends to be overcome with boredom as we lay dormant. Although some prefer the peace and quiet, there are others, such as myself, filled with energy and longing for new things to happen in life. I am usually a bored person and I am speaking from my perspective when I want something new to do. I currently work two jobs and am studying two different courses. All because I want the hours of my day to be filled with tasks and that I should not lack in purpose. When we do not feed ourselves with newer experiences or stimulus, we begin to tire of seeing the same thing every day. We begin to dread waking up and knowing that we have to observe and participate in the same routine, in which we once found joy and satisfaction but no longer. The longing for something new pushes us out of our comfort zones and tend to revitalize our spirits as we set out to do something new, and something which would stimulate us.

Whether challenging or not, there is awesome joy which comes from the exhilarating adventure in which we partake in. Before we set our eyes on conquering what lays beyond the horizon, let us first conquer our unwillingness to grow in experience and surpass the self-created boundaries of our comfort zone. I constantly dream of invigorating my mind with various outlooks on different opportunities the world has to offer. I dream high and big about the places I want to go, the people I want to meet. I wish to sojourn in different places with different atmospheres and want to settle somewhere which fills my heart with peace. The world has a hidden beauty to it. Take a look at the natural geographical sights. The way in which they have been fashioned. Or look at the ancient constructs, which ancient hands have built with technology far ahead of their time. Isn't there more you want to see? I wish to captivate my mind by purposing myself with finding a new habitat. The present domain is outgrowing me and my desire to remain fades more and more each day. I seek to run far and wide according to the will of feeding my mind. To find the hidden meaning of my life, I must look for myself in different areas, doing something different. I must discover and I must overcome. I am tired of never changing. I grow weary of remaining in the same location doing the same things. For some reason, nothing suffices where I am in situated in my work and personal life. The reality of life, which seems to me, is acquiring sufficient personal finances to create something new. Everything costs money! I have set myself a vision of what I want to do and am determined to get through it step by step. I must remain patient and many times I get discouraged. Yet, I have to remind my brain that in order to succeed, a plan must be formulated and that things in this world take time. I have constructed a plan, stuck by it thus far, and will follow it religiously to see my goals achieved. Yet, at the same time, I also want something different. What is that hole in my heart? I care to fill it. With many attempts I have attempted to fill that vacuum but to no avail. I was made to believe that there is only so much you can do, but was wrong. I hope to partake in something different. May my cup run over with adventures of a lifetime, to create everlasting stories in which I can serve some purpose to a bigger picture.

III

Disappointingly, the grass is not always greener on the other side. When you attempt to try something different or move into a new field of work, there are going to be challenges. These are simply the dynamics of being constantly kinetic in your placement in life. Life is a motion and you will always be on the move. Allow these motions to take you through vast locations and great experiences. 'Go with the flow'. When you trample upon a new adventure, there come with it; new obstacles and the consequences which follow thereafter. You should not hold yourself back because if you do, how else do you expect to grow mentally. It's the experiences we accumulate that morph us into who we are. As you know, I have spoken multiple times about my army experiences and the challenges I faced, but now I want to share with you my prison experience. When I concluded my service term in Singapore, I moved back to Melbourne in August 2018 and began looking for a job. I needed a source of income on a casual basis because I was about to pursue my full-time education in university. I could not commit to studying and working full-time. I stumbled upon a job opportunity in a prison as a Correctional Officer. Upon reflection, I decided that this job would suit my personality and contribute well to my resume, for the sake of my future goals. It would do me well to gain experience in this industry and I felt that it suited my long-term purpose. I had not done anything like this before but I was encouraged to pursue it. I succeeded in the recruitment stages and found myself working in the prison service merely two months thereafter.

With every new beginning, you can only prepare yourself to an extent until you actually know what the path ahead of you consists of. You then determine whether this is a suitable choice for yourself. I did not overthink it and decided to try something new, so I went along for the ride. I began to understand what my job entailed and the responsibilities that I was burdened with. I was respectful of the job and I sought to see through my duties to the best of my abilities. As I write this, I am currently still employed as a Correctional Officer and possess roughly two and half years of experience. I remember vaguely at the start of the job I considered quitting, not because I was scared of the prisoners, but because I was newly aware of the stress that the job entailed. Months later I realized I was losing myself and I was becoming frequently suicidal, for reasons unknown to me. I suspected that it was rooted from extensive hours in a negative environment. Rather, I saw this as an opportunity to sharpen my people skills. I saw a bravery in myself when dealing with prisoners who would be oppressive. I realized that I was not afraid and willing to be stern when prisoners would display aggressive behaviour. I determined that I would not be moved with insults or abusive behaviour, rather I would take a stand and reinforce my sense of pride. I would not back down and this exposure through time has removed my fear of man. I am no longer afraid to speak out and be assertive in my personal life and I have the prison experience to thank for that. More time passed but I saw myself growing bitter. I committed a lot of time to working and making money, but at the cost of what? My mental health? I realized that I was beginning to jeopardize my state of mind and at times, you need to relent from harshness.

This was taking me downhill but I accustomed to recalling the positive occurrences in my life and frequent prayer before entering work. I was going to be working in what seemed like another world temporarily and that it would contribute positively to my list of experiences. This is all contributing towards an end goal and there is a purpose for my placement in life at present. I understood the concept that it was for my future and with that headspace was enabled to continue working in that environment. I had to gauge external stimuli and positive thoughts which would bring me happiness. I made valuable friendships with numerous staff and that assisted me to press on the rigorous hours of the day. At this stage, I still do not have a clear answer as to why I seem to feel suicidal at my workplace. At times, I feel left out and alone, which causes me to slumber back into the negativity that I so desperately run away from. I still deal with my personal issues in the workplace, yet I strive forward. I know that all of this will account for something when I have met my end goal. I constantly reflect on the lessons I have learnt through my past experiences. I know that I am not afraid of anyone and have the confidence of standing up for myself. After all, prisoners are also humans, not the monster from our nightmares. They can be pacified, but not always with force, with words. This is an ability I found in myself. I have also developed further confidence to look after myself. Being in a critical environment where anything can happen, I realized that I am able to keep my guard up. When incidents took place, I was always ready to deal with them.

These skills that I have adopted can be applied to instances in the real world. Working in a prison has made me a stronger person mentally and I have expanded my state of mind and toughened up. I am inclined to mention that the psychology behind it is continuously being exposed to unwanted or undesired stimuli until you begin to accept it and overcome it. This is an example of the beauty of challenges.

IV

I noticed that I have edified my ability to be self-controlled. Self-control is a state of mind which is a wise ability to possess because can save you from jumping into dangerous potholes in life. Discipline supports your mind to understand what is good for you and what is not, you begin to develop wisdom in this area and start to make more responsible choices. I developed this through reflecting on the reasons why people end up in prisons. I reflected on their stories and their attributes which contributed to their incarceration. I realized that they although they might not have had much in life, they still chose the easy route and found themselves incarcerated for their wrong decisions. I sought to never be like that because the easy way is not always the correct way. I realized that I was fortunate to have more in life, with a sustained background so I decided that whilst working in the prison I wanted to do something else that would fulfill my desire of wanting more. I felt that prison work was too easy and it was not testing me enough. Yes, I developed those skills I mentioned, but they were not always being tested and refined with iron. This is where I stumbled upon my second job; Residential Youth Worker. I sought this opportunity as I understood that I would be serving the disadvantaged youth of society. These are innocent children whom I felt immense sorrow for after hearing of their childhood experiences. I decided that if I could make a difference somewhere, this would be a good place to start. I saw that I could actively contribute in assisting an innocent child pursue a better lifestyle. If I could help to open doors for these children, I was going to be an efficient door man. As I write presently, I commenced my job as a Youth Worker job in January 2021. I am new to this and I am beginning to find my footing in two different roles at the same time. With my final year of education at university, I decided that I could do roles for a living until I would finish my studies at the end of 2021.

V

Being in the child protection field, I learnt a lot about the youth who had come from a disadvantaged background. My role is to assist the youth individually to adapt a positive outlook on life on a daily basis by taking them to appointments and actively participating with them in activities that contribute to their well-being and mental health. My influence on them must be positive and for the youth to develop their character. Although I only started recently, I opened my eyes to the possibility that I could make a difference in their lives. To watch them smile as we play games or relate to them on a serene walk in the park. I saw that carrying out these works enabled me to overcome myself in always being negative, as I was put in a position to be a conduit for joy. In such a way, I looked at it as training for my mind to radiate positive energy and to pass it on to others. The happiness that I share with the youth is meaningful and has the power to make a difference. Now I understand that this skill of creating positivity as a means of support, is being practiced in my workplace but can be used in my personal life and in different situations. The reason I am doing this is to give a hopeful perspective for the one disadvantaged, yet I myself am being encouraged and strengthened through my work. It seems that it works both ways.

VI

At the start of this chapter, I was talking about exploring the world. I was talking about the physical sense, yet I was alluring to the exploration of oneself. We are like the world we live in. We hold the beauty and the hidden concepts of the world and there are many things in us which we can impart to others. We can share our own knowledge and experiences with people from different cultural and diverse backgrounds. Our own roads can be bridged to the roads of others and in turn, others can share and we can learn from them as well. Through my work experiences, I have conquered myself and my emotions. I have strengthened my mental intuitive. I have trained my mind to observe the positive and that all I do, has some purpose behind it. For the good of others, or myself, I strive forward to take the next step in the development of myself and the ability to resonate with my experiences allows them to mold me as a person and to be stronger. I have acquired knowledge and wisdom through my work and now possess skills I never saw myself having before. I challenged myself to seek out the things which were hidden within myself and have put them into practice. The reality of exploration is that although there are hidden challenges and darker paths, you gain knowledge and wisdom and therefore expand your state of mind to cope with the larger schemes of existence.

It does not stop here though. Each day that I attend both of my workplaces, I continuously sharpen my skills. I am tested and my knowledge is expanded. I see through the vines, something greater for achievement. Though I may stumble through suicidal ideation or loneliness, I have trained my mind to focus on my goals. In this sense, I overcome negativity every day. I broaden my experiences so that I may contribute to the future with efficiency and patience. The challenges which I face are iron which sharpen my being which is also iron.

"Iron sharpens iron..."- Proverbs 27:17

10

ACTA NON VERBA

"......be courageous and act."- Ezra 10:4

I

One of the things in life which routinely disappoints me is when people say things without taking action. I don't just appreciate lip service, but I would rather if someone meant what they said and physically carried out their promise. It is a disappointment to have held such an expectation but only to be let down or to be kept waiting and waiting; to be led on and the action never comes. Sadly, this is the way of some people. I have learnt not to expect much in life and whatever happens, will happen. Even in situations when I am dealing with businesses or waiting to hear a response about an item that I was looking forward to purchase; we are not always met with the expected outcome. There are times in life where we are at our lowest and this is when we become vulnerable. Extreme vulnerability lowers our self-esteem which in turn forces us to depend on a person, object or event to keep our moods elevated. Nothing is certain, and everything is susceptible to go wrong. We are not the authors of our fate and the circumstances around us are not in our control. We must not expect too much from life or from people. Sometimes we should not even expect from ourselves.

When I was in the army, I went in with the mindset that I was going to excel and be a commanding officer. The Officer Cadet course was a grueling nine-month course which trained you to be a leader of a platoon or a company of soldiers. Before you could master soldiers, you were required to master yourself. I saw this as an opportunity to want to make my parents proud. Imagine being in a charge of a company of men. With the solid bar signifying the rank, came with it the command of utmost respect. If you were an officer, you were a leader. This course was only going to be opened to the soldiers who performed exceptionally well during the three- month Basic Military Training. During BMT, we gained knowledge of this course and the requirements of us, should we be willing to transition after our BMT. I told myself that I was going to aim for it. All was well, until I reached a stumbling block which caused me to fall out of my BMT. I mentioned in an earlier chapter of the personal psychological issues I faced whilst in the army and till this day, it seems to haunt me that I gave in to those issues and I beat myself for not being strong enough. To think back, I could have smashed out the courses with the mental capacity I have now and if I could go back. However, I expected too highly of myself. I did not realize the mental strength that was required for the course. It is not something they touched much on in the army. Not only was the physical aspect important, but mainly the mental. I could not even finish my BMT, how was I ever going to get to OCS? With my expectations not being met, I began to feel vulnerable. I simply had to drop out. The questions I keep asking myself cause me to wish that I was stronger back then. I am confident that if I started this training again by some chance, I would excel now only because I have trained my mind to be resistant to isolation and adjustment issues. We are not always going to meet our own expectations and standards and this showed me how much I actually disappointed myself, and the long-lasting impact it has had on me till now. I said to myself over and over that I was going to go ahead and do it, but my actions failed me and in turn failed myself. I learnt now that when I say I am going to do something; I am going to see it through till the end. I have ensured of this self-practice till this day and learnt this only after my grueling failure to challenge myself.

It is easy to make a promise and not keep it. After all, we are humans. I am reluctant to expect much or trust that situations would pan out the way I imagined. It is only through grievous encounters of expectations not being met that has forced me to conjure such a personality type in which I am slow to trust. We must not lean on the nature of man or materialistic items as nothing is yet perfected. We are all in a sandbox where we are testing the waters and experimenting with different outcomes. Could you blame the human race? Selfish desires steal away good intentions to make good on the promises which are made to us and then we act as though the world is coming to an end when they are not met. Are we serious? What else did you expect? I am not saying that we should immediately doubt everyone or anything but allow space in your conscience to bear the credibility of things not working out nor coming to pass. Sincerely, I say, the nature of this world is deceit. Not everything that is promised to you is true. Lies exist in the midst of us and they have been around since our creation. The object of the liar is to deliver you into a trap of vulnerability in which you begin to lose the ability to distinguish true and false. When you are confused, you are open to be swayed by that which sounds "valid" and "promising" enough for you to drop your whole life and run ten thousand miles just because you feel with your bones that what is mentioned is the ultimate truth. Has that truth been put to the test? Does your mind validate what it receives and then believes? Or does everything sound too good to be true yet desirable, that you would drop everything and pursue it? I tell you, it does not end well for this person who does not test the truth, for they could be running their whole lives and not meet what they have been promised. Do not expect, rather, turn to the meaning of your own life and create expectations by yourself, for yourself! You know yourself well enough to avoid what disappoints you personally. Have mercy on yourself and when you have done so, act upon the self-love and goodwill that is so necessary in your life.

II

Nothing is at it seems in this world. If things are too good to be true, in most cases they are. I have been a subject of foolishness an extensive number of times and sometimes it takes a while to learn things. It can require a series of hard events to eventually screw your head on right and then you begin to realize what you have been doing wrong the whole time. Regrettably, all the time spent in the wrong relationship or investing in the wrong things in life has been lost for good, however, the good news comes from the knowledge you have acquired and move on with the understanding of what you mean to look for in the future. You should dictate the path ahead by expecting yourself to learn from your mistakes. One thing about setting expectations is that you set a standard for yourself to meet. A standard may be too high for some to reach. You will never have your ideal standard met so why set the bar up in the first place. Just make life work for yourself and ensure your own happiness. In that sense, you will rarely have disappointment. Expectations have the capability to alter our realities so much so that we allow our expectations to overrule our emotions and the right to choose what it best for ourselves. Our expectations override our will and choices the more we cave into them. As we know, expectations can destroy our happiness to a degree for the following reasons:

1) **We expect that our life should be fair.** This is not the case and it never will be. There will always be the occurrence of unfortunate events which will happen to good people. There is never a reason for this nor an explanation. This is the way life is. You must share the sunshine with the rain that comes with it. You deny the experience of being a human if you think that bad things will never happen. After all, we live in a cruel world; just be the best version of yourself.

2) **We expect everyone to share the same values and harbor the same kindness as we do.** Not everyone has the same heart as you. This is also not the case because everyone has been raised with a different upbringing, therefore inhibiting a different mindset to how they view life. Not everyone will be as kind or loving as you are. You should just focus on those who care of you and earning the acceptance of those you like. Do not go too much out of your way of people who will never appreciate you. Believe me, it is not worth it.

3) **We expect everyone to agree with our opinions and views.** This absolutely cannot be so. There would not be any wars or conflicts if this was the case. The world was meant to be a peaceful place upon creation but thereafter it, there came too may conflicting personalities in society for the peace to continue. Not everyone is going to agree with what you must say or the way you do things, nevertheless, do not let that

hinder you from doing your best and remaining true to yourself.

4) **We expect people to understand what we are talking about or what we are going through.** Everyone has a different understanding on the way things work in life and the circumstances which occur shape the way that they understand things. Not everyone is on the same boat of experiences, so you cannot expect people to feel what you feel and experience what you experience. You need to seek out and mingle with likeminded people. The good news is there are a lot of people out there who a longing to be understood, just like you.

5) **We expect ourselves to perform to the best of our abilities every time we attempt something.** We believe that because we possess the skills to do something, we can do it to the best of our abilities. Those who practice perfectionism can never expect to be satisfied because nothing is indeed perfect! It is good to set standards but everyone is human and there will always be off days in which you will simply not perform as good as you expected on any given task. It is alright to falter at some points but it does not change your worth. You are only human. Learn from your mistakes and attempt your task through different approaches.

6) **We expect materials or success to bring us happiness.** Not every situation you›re involved in or every object that you purchase is going to satisfy you. Materialism does not get you far as there will be something created afterwards which will surpass the value of what you have purchased. You must create

your own happiness in your circumstances and be grateful for what you still have. It is good to attribute wealth but only with the correct mindset, can you manage it effectively to contribute to the fullness of your life. Reflect on your blessings regardless the situations.

III

I propose that potentially, saving yourself from expectations in life may be cultivating gratitude. If you think that humanity is all good and capable, you will always be frustrated as the perfect society does not exist, nor do perfect people. If you however, train your mind to think otherwise, then potentially you will discover joy every time you surprise yourself when your abilities surpass your expectations. It takes a bit of reverse psychology.

Learn to expect the situation for what presently is, rather than what it should be. When you learn to let go of your unrealistic expectations, an open road unfolds right in front of you.

Instead of expecting situations to occur, learn to create your own situations which can fulfil your desires. The human mind is built to hold a vast amount of knowledge and it holds the capability for creation and imagination. Use these skills to create the expectations which cater to you personally. Interpret this how you will, but it would be helpful to give this a try. Train your mind to avoid disappointment as much as you can.

A long train of disappointment can lead to absolute discouragement and cause you to never finding peace in yourself. Being constantly disappointed can ruin your relationships and the bridges of trust that you have built with others. It may not always be your fault, but it would assist you in looking at disappointments in a different light. Use them to motivate you to look for better things in life. You do not always want to be upset about the same thing. You do not want to give up on your hobbies or the things you love doing just because you expected approval from others. People have different tastes and you must accept that. Celebrate with those who celebrate you! When I expected people to care about my interests, it did not always happen. Their heart was not in the same place as mine was. If I do not receive the same efforts I am putting out, I have learnt to disengage and stick to myself. I want to remain true to myself first so that it will hinder my expectation levels of others. I realized that if I could help myself first, I can save myself a lot of wasted time and effort relying on circumstances that would not benefit me anyways. Life is too short to seek the approval of others. You need to create your own joy and pursue the things that you want to do. Only you know what is best for yourself and you must not fear doing things to help yourself. Do not worry about third party opinions! After all, their opinions do not count unless you allow them to. A lot of people do not realize that they get disappointed because they allow themselves to be. It is how you perceive these things which can help or burden you. It is up to you at the end of the day. If your mind can conceive negativity, then it can also conceive positivity. Do not wait for others to approve of you, approve yourself!

IV

People tend to avoid disappointment more than other emotions. Disappointments bring about the most grief and the greatest onslaught of hopelessness. This brings me to discuss hopelessness. Disappointments lead to hopelessness if the emotions from the affliction are not managed effectively. I understand this form of hopelessness because I have been through it constantly. When you look out at a dark gloomy day, with sadness in mind, and see that you do not have much to do or be involved in, you lose sight of what the future holds and disregard all hope. Losing your hope in people is so easy when people fail to regard you, or forget to contact you. When you ask them to do something and they do not make time for it. They might not see your needs as important, compared to how you may view it, which means that they might not get around to supporting your needs in time. This alleviates their status as unreliable and you might never understand their reasoning for the way they do things. You will always have the desire to receive an explanation but I learned early in life, that sometimes people will do things for odd reasons and you may never ever understand why they do it or their motives. You might never receive any explanations and you will have to accept that for the rest of your life. I had friends walk out on me and lose touch with me for no reason. One day, they stopped speaking to me, and I never knew why. It hurts yes, but I just had to continue on without them because time waits for no man. I received no closure from them and had to find something to fill the vacant hole they left in my heart. People will not treat you the same way as you treat them. This is simply because people hold different values as you. People can tend to be selfish towards your needs but you will have to accept it. Do not be discouraged though because you are still in charge of your life. You still have the ability to progress and take hold of the changes in your life. In this day and age, the world has grown cold. Truth be told, despite being advised to not worry, at times I sit and wonder why things are the way they are. I cannot comprehend yet I determine myself to stumble across some answer that could potentially explain the reasons for the way people behave or the way circumstances unfold. Truth be told, I do not know. I may never know. If you hold a simple view towards life and take things easily, you might find it easier to manage your issues. Ensure that you do not lose yourself in a downwards spiral due to disappointment or anger. Somethings in the universe are not meant to be answered and the explanations we seek for the way things are, may never exist. Just live your life and look after yourself regardless.

"I consider that our present sufferings are not comparable to the glory that will be revealed in us." - Romans 8:18

11

OUR MARK

"I have fought the good fight, I have finished the race, I have kept the faith." – 2 Timothy 4:7

I

As the days go by, I sit idly and whilst being mindful, notice the ambience of the sky which reflect the moods of the weather. Day after day, time continues. The birds continue to chirp and the howl of the wind seeps through me as I stand before the light of the sun, questioning whether I have done enough. Have I finished what I have set out to do? The question revolves around my mind and causes me to reflect on it over and over. I am mindful of the slow and long breaths I take as my mind carries me to question myself. Was I doing the right thing all along? I am caught in the gap of ending it or pressing forward. The birds continue to chirp and I finally decide that I am ready. It must end, as all things do.

In the present, I go about my routine of work, studies and socialization. Whilst taking part in this, I still feel that something is lacking. I am not sure what it is but I feel as though I have not yet achieved something. Maybe in the current space of time, I am at a standstill in the crossroads of which part I should choose next. I contemplate what I am to do next. I continuously brainstorm different opportunities that I can create but I forget that I must move with time and wait upon God to present me with the right opportunities at the right time. So, I recline and remind myself, that patience is a virtue, all the while wrestling with my active mind to stay calm and wait. I need to continue my works somehow. I am wrestling with my mind, day in and day out. Constantly vigilant of something which can captivate me and put my mind at ease, with the assurance that I am going to do something good for the human race. I strive to benefit and make changes in the lives of others wherever I can, however I can.

What I have left in myself now is the urge to do something new. I do not know what is next but I will use whatever *opportunity I have to endeavor on a new adventure. My state of mind presently is hungry and thirsty for something which it can chew on. Something nutritious and of good value. I must feed my mind with the things that can benefit my soul, as does every other person.*

II

We should always strive to do something creative. We should not sit back in our personal bubble for an extensive amount of time, lest we get too comfortable but we should create a new adventure or a hobby. As an altruist, I seek to help others in any way that I can. I am always looking for someone to share my love and care with. This helps me to be fulfilled and it is not for a personal gain. My mind keeps going in circles though. As long as I let it sit idly, the darkness comes and throws me in a pit, where I have to climb out. This is a repeated cycle for as long as I can remember and I am still working on breaking it. The thoughts of the darkness still visit me but I have found that sharing it all the more has helped me to fight back and inscribing it in some text has allowed me to endure. This has taught me that we need to take our miseries out on something. We should vent it out in some way that would benefit us and not harm others either. This exhibits a healthy state of mind.

No doubt there will always be challenges, but isn't this why we continue? To overcome is our innate reaction and we learn from our experiences. Life is the best teacher and how we live does not allude much from a textbook, but rather derived from past experiences and the advice of our elders. Whilst we are young and full of energy, we need to keep doing things that we will thank ourselves for in the long run. Do not let emotions hinder you, take risks and do something that you never thought you could do. I never thought I could write a book but almost twenty-nine thousand words later, here I am. When you dedicate yourself to some activity or recreation, you allow yourself to discover your strengths and weaknesses. This can give you the opportunity to improve yourself and open the doors to discovering more of yourself. Seek out your path and work out your purpose. Set and example to others and demonstrate that you can also overcome your challenges. Someone out there is looking up to you. Someone out there is striving to be like you, set a good example and be an inspiration to yourself and others.

You might feel that no one cares about your progress, but at times even I have to remind myself that I am doing this for my sake. After all, no one else is living my life. I am accountable for what I do.

III

You have all the capabilities in your soul to create an everlasting saga of your life. I challenge you to make something out of it. Do not sell out, but through your grit and efforts, fine tune yourself and achieve what you want to achieve. Set your eyes out on the horizon and tell yourself that you are going to be a better person than you were yesterday. The human mind is able to adapt and overcome, so stretch your limits. No matter how old you are, you can make a difference, as long as you have the right mindset to take control over your emotions and actions. It is never too late to start improving yourself and overcoming what hinders you. At times I still make battle with the darkness, but I have to continue to conquer myself. I have to continue to stretch my boundaries. Every day I have to keep pushing through. I have to keep devising strategies on how I am going to deal with myself. The task at hand is not easy but I have to be responsible for it. We have to believe in ourselves that we can continue to push forward in hard times. We have to lean on ourselves and take care of ourselves. I learned at times that in instances where no one could understand what I was going through, I had to be there for myself. I practice self-care and remind myself of the blessings I still have the yet to come. We all have a reason or some motivation to push forward and continue. Identify them! Identify what empowers you to get out of bed each morning and make the day ahead filled with achievements and serenity.

There will always be times when you may not be able to get out feeling refreshed, yet you need to push through. As you move forward, the light at the end of the tunnel is only coming closer and closer. You are making yourself stronger with each step and are learning, through firsthand experience, how to keep yourself on the path. Daily, this is what I have manage. I must regulate my thoughts and my emotions and be mature in my approach. If needed, I have to disregard my emotions and set my priorities straight. What needs to be done has to be done, regardless! Listen to your heart. In each of us, there is always going to be a longing for something that will bring us happiness. We may not always know what it is, but as you continue in this journey of life, you will find it, and with it, everything else. I am in the constant pursuit of happiness and although being happy is a state of mind. It is also a full-fledged journey. Brave your obstacles and reach your end goal. You are made for more!

IV

I reflect now on my destiny. I have to meet my destiny. It is not coming to me; I must go and grab it. I have to ensure that I take the right steps because I know I have made many mistakes in life which have caused me to stumble off the path into a sequence of immense suffering. I am still learning to cope with the regrets of my past and the one way I know how to move on from them, is to learn from my mistakes. It seems as though mistakes shape us into being defined as the people we are today. Do not fret, mistakes are not the end. You live and you learn. I notice that I am living an ordinary life but I want to make it extraordinary! I want to be something big one day. I have set this goal in my heart and am working cautiously to complete it. It is based on my perspective of this goal which will dictate whether I reach it. Marcus Aurelius, an esteemed emperor of Rome said "Everything we see is a perspective, not the truth.". My situations are not true unless I make them to be so. The stoic philosopher has imparted in me the wisdom to identify the perspectives I want to adopt upon my life in order for me to be successful. We make our own success and we will not always be celebrated by others. Worry not, as long as you are happy, what else matters? You have to celebrate yourself and your own achievements.

The world we live in will constantly remind you of who you are meant to be despite your personal desires. It will force you to conform to its standards when you were born to be something different. Our state of mind may feel attacked when we speak out about our own desires and receive backlash in return, but you must continue to speak. There is nothing wrong with being different. It is about time the world was introduced to something new. I will caution you, however, that if you speak out, do so with respect of others' views and thoughts and you will have the respect of others in turn. Not all views and ideals will be accepted, but provided they have good intentions, stick to them and work them out. In time, people will come to understand and appreciate what you have to share.

Remember that if you have goodness in you, you are a light to this world. The world needs more light. It has grown cold long before you or I were born. So, all the more, we must impart our goodness into the world so that people will know that good still exists. Do not run from persecution! Stand your ground and back yourself up. Turn the other cheek, and the respect of the world will be yours. Mahatma Gandhi said "The true measure of any society can be found in how it treats its most vulnerable members". Are you going to look after the vulnerable? Help the sick, give to the poor, have mercy on the lesser. Allow your mind to be overcome with goodness; that you need to pour out your goodness on others because you cannot contain it. Be an example that society will follow.

Instruct your mind to follow goodness and your body and soul will follow along. As much as you want for all problems in life to end, it will not be the case, but if you can combat darkness with light, then you will have won the battle and the war. We are conquerors. Nothing is too difficult for us to overcome. Accept that and wear it proudly. You are strong and determined and nothing will stop you. Ensure that you have your priorities straight and do not be tempted off the path. You have one life to make is as good as you can. Do not waste time pursuing other desires which you leave you in a state of regret and rob you of your joy. Time cannot be bought back. Your days are numbered and there is only so much that you can do. As long as you do your best, that is sufficient.

Remember, it all comes down to your state of mind and your perspective in life. Keep your mind open and your heart ready to take on any circumstance. When you have met your goals, you will know that you have won.

"Not all of us can do great things. But we can do small things with great love."- Mother Teresa

EPILOGUE

Dear reader,

If you have made it this far into the journey of the book, sincerely: I thank you. Thank you for reading and getting to know who I am, what I am, what I have gone through and the events which shaped me into the person I am today. I have no doubt that you will take something away from this book in some way or another. And even if you did not, that is alright, it means the world to me that you even looked at the first page.

I created this project in hopes that I could make a difference and shed light on what life has taken me through. I believe that I have shared enough and am unsure if I am satisfied but I do know that I have been open and transparent with you. I do not feel well to end this book but all things must come to an end. Although I feel some part of myself being torn away as I put this to a close, I feel that I might have something else to create in the future.

I know that our minds are constantly being reshaped based on the circumstances which occur in our life. The rollercoaster of emotions all humans go through in their life reminds us that we are humans. We feel, we love, we care and we share.

We need to speak our minds and align our hearts with what we think. Pursue your dreams and make good of the opportunities presented to you. Be strong in your heart and take a hold of your life. You are strong and special; you have a purpose.

Remember, take control of your mind and create the most exciting journey you can ever create. I hope that I have made an impact.

My hopes and dreams travel with you.

With love,
Keshan Singh

"You have power over your mind - not outside events. Realize this, and you will find strength."

- Marcus Aurelius

www.ingramcontent.com/pod-product-compliance
Lightning Source LLC
Chambersburg PA
CBHW031339060726
47590CB00007B/2544